Math Workstations in Action

Learn how to incorporate math workstations into your elementary math classes. Math workstations allow students to engage in meaningful, independent math practice through student-driven games and activities, and can be implemented as part of a math workshop or in a traditional math class. In this book, bestselling author and consultant Nicki Newton shows you how to set up and manage math workstations for topics such as fluency, word problems, math vocabulary, and more. You'll also learn how to differentiate the activities for all ability levels and promote rigorous instruction, enabling your students to get the most out of this fun and engaging instructional method. Topics include:

- Teaching fractions, decimals, measurement, geometry, and more with a variety of tools and hands-on activities;
- Developing word problems and games to help students gain understanding of difficult mathematical concepts;
- Using precise mathematical language to encourage clear communication and logical thinking;
- Evaluating student competency and development with pre-assessments, anecdotals, checklists, and self-reflections;
- Implementing new technologies to think through, explain, and present mathematical concepts.

Each chapter includes a variety of charts, tools, and practice problems that you can use in the classroom immediately, and the strategies can be easily adapted for students at all levels of math fluency across grades 3–5.

Dr. Nicki Newton has been an educator for 28 years, working both nationally and internationally, with students of all ages. She has worked on developing Math Workshop and Guided Math Institutes around the country; visit her website at www.drnickinewton.com. She is also an avid blogger (www.guidedmath.wordpress.com), tweeter (@drnickimath), and Pinterest pinner (www.pinterest.com/drnicki7).

Also Available from Dr. Nicki Newton

(www.routledge.com/eyeoneducation)

Guided Math in Action: Building Each Student's Mathematical
Proficiency with Small-Group Instruction

Math Workshop in Action: Strategies for Grades K–5

Math Running Records in Action: A Framework
for Assessing Basic Fact Fluency in Grades K–5

Math Problem Solving in Action: Getting Students
to Love Word Problems, Grades 3–5

Math Problem Solving in Action: Getting Students
to Love Word Problems, Grades K–2

Math Workstations in Action

Powerful Possibilities for Engaged Learning in Grades 3–5

Dr. Nicki Newton

Routledge
Taylor & Francis Group

NEW YORK AND LONDON

First published 2018
by Routledge
711 Third Avenue, New York, NY 10017

and by Routledge
2 Park Square, Milton Park, Abingdon, Oxon, OX14 4RN

Routledge is an imprint of the Taylor & Francis Group, an informa business

Library of Congress Cataloging-in-Publication Data
A catalog record for this book has been requested

ISBN: 978-1-138-67502-5 (hbk)
ISBN: 978-1-138-67503-2 (pbk)
ISBN: 978-1-315-56091-5 (ebk)

Typeset in Palatino and Formata
by Apex CoVantage, LLC

Printed and bound in the United States of America by Sheridan

Dedication

To Gregory G. County, beloved uncle

Contents

Foreword

Math Workstations in Action: Powerful Possibilities for Engaged Learning in Grades 3–5 is a powerful, informative, and practical journey through a framework for designing and implementing workstations in a math workshop or guided math classroom. Broadly and consistently implementing the ideas, games, and management techniques presented in *Math Workstations in Action* can change teachers' view of using stations in the 3–5 grade level while engaging students in intentional mathematical learning.

The number one question that intermediate teachers ask about implementing guided math and math workshops in their math classrooms is "What do all the other students do while I teach small groups of students?" When they hear that the answer is workstations, they think to themselves, "We don't do stations in the upper grades!" Well, Dr. Nicki Newton will change their mind as she shares her many practical, classroom-tested strategies and math activities to convince teachers to do just that! We know that managing a math workshop classroom can be challenging, but whether you are trying math workshop for the first time or are a seasoned guided math teacher you will find many effective ways to create self-directed learning during your workstation time in this book. Math workstations are intentionally planned by the teacher and always with the students in mind. They are a place for every student to productively practice the mathematics they have learned.

Done well, there is something so engaging, mathematically rich, and even magical about math workshop. Teachers facilitating differentiated small group lessons while all the other students are mathematically engaged and challenged with intentionally planned and teacher-created workstations offers students the ability to have choice in deepening their math knowledge. Everything we know about student learning and classroom practice tells us that differentiating student learning is crucial. We know that students who work at their level of ability and interest are engaged and learn new concepts more deeply and retain those concepts longer. We have seen that students who work in pairs and small groups learn to listen to others, ask insightful and respectful questions, and become reflective of their own mathematical understandings. All of the reasons listed above, and presented in this book, will assist teachers at all levels in discovering ways to engage students to work autonomously at math workstations.

Dr. Nicki reminds us all in Part I that workstations work toward a common goal for all of us, a balanced math program with engaging, purposeful practice opportunities that are framed by State Standards. It is one thing to hope for this to happen in a teacher's classroom. It's quite another to propose and describe practical management techniques and engaging activities that are student-tested and easy to implement for any teacher when managing workstations. That is exactly why this resource is so helpful. Part II of *Math Workstations in Action* models many effective techniques of implementing mathematical activities that enable students to be autonomous learners while practicing the four "must-have" workstations: basic fact fluency, solving word problems, math journaling, and using digital technology. In Part III, the book offers specific activities for many tricky topics found in grades 3–5. Specifically, place value, fractions, decimals, measurement, and geometry. Sprinkled throughout the book you will find sample anchor charts, task cards, reflective exit tickets for stations, and charts to help you roll out workstations. These will get every teacher started with a collection of effective workstations. Not only that, it will trigger every teacher's mind as to what other workstations they might create and incorporate throughout the year. Part IV offers numerous ways to assess student work when they are not with the teacher. Use of daily and weekly reflection cards and ways students can self-assess are included in this section. Every teacher will find that math workstations must be engaging, interactive, standards-based, rigorous, and differentiated, and students must be held accountable for their learning during this important purposeful practice. All of these topics are discussed with classroom-tested examples throughout the book.

Math Workstations in Action will help teachers create classrooms where all of your students are engaged in mathematical discovery and practice in ways that will help them see themselves as mathematicians, who are always at work. You will want to continually revisit the structure that Dr. Nicki offers in this book to plan your next set of workstations, work toward building and maintaining a strong community of mathematical thinkers, use the tools, create task cards, and continue to use the examples to create new and engaging math workstations. Using *Math Workstations in Action* in your classroom will guide you toward meeting your mathematical goals as well and meet the diverse needs of each and every one of your students. You will be working together to achieve mathematical understanding for ALL!

—Dr. Barbara Blanke, Math Educator,
Author, and Consultant

Meet the Author

Dr. Nicki Newton has been an educator for 27 years, working both nationally and internationally, with students of all ages. Having spent the first part of her career as a literacy and social studies specialist, she built on those frameworks to inform her math work. She believes that math is intricately intertwined with reading, writing, listening, and speaking. She has worked on developing math workshop and guided math institutes around the country. Most recently, she has been helping districts and schools nationwide to integrate their State Standards for Mathematics and think deeply about how to teach these within a Math Workshop Model.

Dr. Nicki works with teachers, coaches, and administrators to make math come alive by considering the powerful impact of building a community of mathematicians that make meaning of real math together. When students do real math, they learn it, they own it, they understand it, and they can do it. Every one of them.

Dr. Nicki's website is www.drnickinewton.com. She is also an avid blogger (www.guidedmath.wordpress.com), tweeter (@drnickimath), and Pinterest pinner (www.pinterest.com/drnicki7).

Acknowledgments

I thank God for helping me to know more and to learn more every day. That is really the cycle of knowing, constantly learning more. Teachers and students make that possible for me every day. I thank them all. I thank my first students and I thank the students and teachers I worked with yesterday and every day. I thank Debbie DeSmith because she sparked learning for me as a new teacher. She sent me to every conference that I could find and wanted to attend. She believed in the value of good professional development. She also planted a seed in me about the possibility of always learning more. I am so thankful to her. I thank Lin Goodwin and Ann Sabatini because they let me explore and practice all these ideas as an instructor at Teachers College so many years ago. I thank Heidi Hayes Jacobs because she mentored me for seven years. She taught me a whole bunch of stuff. One of the things she taught me that I really used in this book is the idea that we are digital citizens and that we need to prepare our students for a world that we can't even imagine. She taught me to do that. I will forever be grateful to her. I will pass it along.

I thank my family for all their encouragement, my brother Marvin and sister Sharon, my Aunty Mary, my Uncle Bill, and my cousin Clinese. I also thank all my nieces, nephews, and cousins that inspire me. I thank my ancestors because I stand on their shoulders: Mom, Pops, Bigmom, Mama Anna. I thank my grandpa because he always said that "Anything you want to know you can learn from a book." That's as true today as it was back in 1965. He always said it. I believed him then and still do today. I thank my family because they are strong people, wonderful human beings that believe in schooling and hard work. They've passed those values on to me, each in their own individual way.

My friends are incredible. They encourage me all the time. They say the right thing at the right time. Brittany is incredible! George, my cousin, is fantastic. Danny is the best! Gabby was great working on this project. Anna and Nancy are incredible. Jon and Genesis are terrific. They help me to build centers and prepare them for the road and online workshops.

I would like to thank Dr. Blanke for taking the time to read the book, provide valuable feedback, and for writing the foreword. I appreciate her taking time out of her very busy schedule to contribute to this work. I would also like to thank Christine King for helping me to embrace technology. She taught me so much math stuff too. She shared a whole lot of her knowledge a whole bunch of times. I will always be grateful to her for that. Lauren is the best editor ever. She is a constant encouragement and essential partner in this process of writing a book. I thank the entire editorial team at Routledge that made the production of this book possible.

Part I
Overview of Math Workstations

1

Getting Started

Math Workstations Are a Place for Purposeful Practice!

Math Workstations: Meaningful Practice

Math workstations are spaces and places for students to practice, to get better at math, to go from good to great in what they are doing. They can be done independently, with partners, or in a group. Math workstations are part of a balanced math program. They are meant for purposeful practice. Math workstations can be done in whatever manner best fits your program. Some teachers do them every day in a math workshop daily model. Other teachers do them two or three times a week and do a traditional classroom model on the other days. Some people do whole class explorations, investigations, and lessons on two days and then workstations and guided math groups on the other three days or vice versa.

The most important thing is to start slow. The first thing that people wonder about is where to start. Start small. State standards should frame workstations. Every state has a fluency standard for each grade and word problems. I always encourage teachers to start with these stations. Then, as the year progresses add other stations.

Getting Started

It is important to plan for at least a 20-day rollout. This is the most important part of ensuring that math workstations actually work out. Students need time to learn the set-up of the math block, how to get along with each other, how to talk with each other, and how to work together. It is important to spend time to teach students how to do each of these things. Then, after time has been spent on community building, there must be time spent on the actual workstations.

Math Workstations: One Essential Element of Math Workshop

Math workstations are an instructional strategy that can be used in different math classroom models. Here I want to discuss how math workstations can be one essential element of a math workshop model (see Figure 1.1). In a math workshop model there are three specific elements of the math block. The first part is the introduction. During this part, there is an opening with fluency energizers and routines. After this, there is a mini-lesson about the big ideas in the current unit of study. The second part is the student activity period. It consists of math workstations and guided math groups. Sometimes during this period the teacher does conferences and interviews while students are doing free choice workstations. Guided math groups are done at the same time that the students are in workstations. One of the groups is with the teacher. The third part is the debrief/share. During this part the teacher and students summarize the learning for the day and oftentimes discuss what is happening in the overall unit.

Figure 1.1

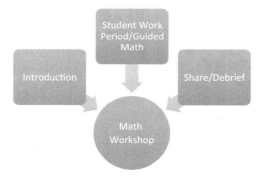

Introducing the Workstations

Remember that the number one rule of workstations is to always teach the workstation to the students before they go there. The teacher should introduce the workstation to the whole class or a small group, depending on the station. If it is a general structure, for example playing Power Towers, then the teacher would teach an easy version of that game to the whole class. Power Towers is a game where students play with small or large cups and are trying to figure out a math problem, such as 4 × 5 (which is often written inside the cup) (the answer is on the bottom so their partners can check). If they get it correct, they get to stack a cup, if not, they just put the cup at the bottom of the pile. Other times, if it is a game that is specific to certain students, then the teacher would teach it to those students in a small group, and once the students have learned it, the game is moved to

Figure 1.2

Rolling Out Math Workstations				
Day	Goal	*I Can* Statement	Practice Activity	Anchor Chart
Monday	Introduce math workstations (general introduction): • What they are. • Why we do them. • When we do them. • How we do them. • Where we do them.	*I can* practice math in workstations.	Dice game	Math workstations introduction.
Tuesday	Introduce math workstations: reading the schedule (look at leveled activities)	*I can* read the math workstation schedule.	Dice game	How do we play dice games?
Wednesday	Introduce math workstations: "What if I get stuck?" board.	*I know* what to do in math workstations.	Domino game	"What if I get stuck?"
Thursday	Introduce individual workstation games and artifact sheets	*I can* work by myself in math workstations.	Domino game	Working with math materials/getting them out and putting them back.
Friday	Practice individual workstation games and artifact sheets	*I can* work by myself in math workstations.	Dice game	Recording my work.
Monday	Introduce partner workstation games and artifact sheets	*I can* work with a partner in math workstations.	Power tower game	Being a good sport.
Tuesday	Practice partner workstation games and artifact sheets	*I can* work with a partner in math workstations.	Board game	How to play a board game.
Wednesday	Introduce group workstation games and artifact sheets	*I can* work with a group in math workstations.	Flashcard game	Being a great group member.
Thursday	Practice group workstation games and artifact sheets	*I can* work with a group in math workstations.	Board game	Math materials.
Friday	Introduce free choice days	*I can* make great choices on math workstation free choice day.	Free choice	How to make good choices on free choice day.

the math workstation. In general, introduce the general game structure to the class and then differentiate in workstations (see Figure 1.2).

Practice Makes Perfect

Many times, teachers will introduce a partner game to the class by having the class split into two groups and calling up people from the groups, so the class is divided into Team A and Team B, and they play against each other. I actually like this model because everyone is playing and engaged and learns the rules. It is also possible to do a fishbowl, where some students come up and play the game and everyone watches and then discusses what happened. The main point here is that students should never be sent to work in a workstation on material that they have never seen or are not ready to do independently.

Four Must-Have Workstations

Workstations are planned at the beginning of each unit. There are some workstations that never change, such as the fluency station, the word problem station, the vocabulary/writing station, and the digital station. However, the work in the stations often changes to reflect the current unit of study. For example, in 3rd grade students might be working on mass or volume word problems during a particular unit of study. In the digital station, they might be working on measurement games, if the unit is around measurement. There is always the Four Must-Have Workstations and then the Unit of Study Workstation (which focuses only on the unit of study) (see Figure 1.3).

Figure 1.3

Four Must-Have Units + Unit of Study				
Fluency	*Word Problems*	*Vocabulary Writing*	*Digital (laptops, desktops, iPods, iPads)*	*Unit of Study (i.e., measurement, fractions, geometry)*
This station focuses on the grade level fluency. So, for example, in 3rd grade some students might still be working on fluency within 20 and 100. This station would have plenty of addition and subtraction games leveled and scaffolded for students to play.	The word problem station focuses on students learning to solve various types of word problems, mainly framed around CGI types and then non-routine problems as well. In this station, students are expected to write as well as solve word problems.	This workstation focuses on vocabulary games for the current unit of study and review of words from past units. In this station, students also work on their interactive math journals and writing prompts about the topic in the current unit of study.	This workstation focuses on teaching the content through 21st century technologies. Students might be playing games on laptops or iPads. They could be working with 3D pens or 3D printers. They are working in the "digital zone" of learning in this space.	This workstation is about the current unit of study. Remember to plan activities that are concrete, pictorial, and abstract.

- I have been rethinking the digital workstation lately. I think you could have a workstation dedicated to technology but you could just as well integrate technology into all the other stations.
- I also have been thinking a great deal about place value as a must-have station that stays up all year so that students build a firm knowledge of place value. Many of the standards require that students do the operations based on place value, properties, and the relationships between the operations. Many students are shaky on place value and have huge gaps from prior grades. In a place value workstation, you could close these gaps by continued practice in engaging ways.

Flexible Groupings

Workstation groupings are flexible (see Figures 1.4, 1.5, and 1.6). Students might work with one set of friends in the fluency station and a completely different set in the digital station. When students are in the workstations they work in a variety of groupings. Some of these groupings are homogeneous and others are heterogeneous. It depends on what the students are doing. When students are practicing their math facts, they are usually in a workstation with others who are working on that same fluency because they need to practice with partners who are working on the same thing. However, at other times, students might be in a heterogeneous group in the vocabulary station playing a game of charades or vocabulary tic-tac-toe. Successful grouping takes planning. But, it is more than possible!

Differentiated/Leveled

Within a math workstation there are many different types of games. For instance, in 3rd grade in the fluency center there will be at least ten addition games. These games are leveled according to different types of strategies and facts that students are working on. Tom might be working out of Bag B, which has Make Ten Facts. Mary might be working out of Bag D, which has Doubles Facts. On an ordinary day, Tom and Mary would be with groups that are working on the same types of facts they are. But, on a free choice day, there are a variety of students in the same center (because students choose where they want to go on these days). So, there must be "Orange Bag Games." Everybody can play these games. They are usually games from the grade below or games from an earlier part of the year that everybody has mastered the concepts. So, in the above scenario, Tom and Mary might play a board game that works on Facts within ten, which would be in the orange bag.

Management/Planning Templates

Figure 1.4

Math Workstation Rotation						
	Fluency	Digital	Word Problems	Unit: Fractions	Writing/ Vocabulary	Guided Math
1st Rotation 8:50–9:05	Group A	Group B	Group C	Group D	Group E	Group F
2nd Rotation 9:05–9:20	Group B	Group A	Group D	Group C	Group F	Group E
3rd Rotation 9:20–9:35	Group E	Group F	Group A	Group B	Group C	Group D

Figure 1.5

Math Workstation Schedule												
	Fluency		Word Problems		Vocabulary/Journals/Writing		Digital		Unit of Study		Guided Math	
Day	R1	R2	R1	R2	R1	R2	R1	R2	R1	R2	R1	R2
Monday	Group 1	Group 2	Group 2	Group 1	Group 3	Group 4	Group 4	Group 3	Group 5	Teacher choice	Teacher choice	Group 5
Tuesday	Group 5	Teacher choice	Group 5	Teacher choice	Group 1	Group 2	Group 2	Group 1	Group 3	Group 4	Group 4	Group 3
Wednesday	Free Choice											
Thursday	Group 3	Group 4	Group 4	Group 3	Group 5	Teacher choice	Group 5	Teacher choice	Group 1	Group 2	Group 2	Group 1
Friday	Group 1	Group 2	Group 2	Group 1	Group 3	Group 4	Group 4	Group 3	Group 5	Teacher choice	Teacher choice	Group 5

Figure 1.6

See this site for management board ideas:
https://www.pinterest.com/drnicki7/management-boardssystems/

Accountability

Teachers often worry that students are going to not do what they are supposed to be doing in the workstation. This could happen. Accept it. Plan for it. That means, spend the time at the beginning of the year teaching students how to play the games, how to record the math from the games, and how to reflect on the games so that they are actually doing what they are supposed to.

Every student should have a center folder where they keep the work they are doing. Mrs. Shannon (2016) suggests having a red sticker on one side and a green sticker on the other side of the folder. On the red side, they put work that they have completed. On the green side, they put work that they are still working on. Many teachers also use sheet protectors, whether they are bought or made with sheet protectors and duct tape, so that students can do their work there and not waste tons of paper. The key here is to tell the students to write their name and to not erase the work. The teacher can then go back and check the work and after it is checked put it in a basket to be cleaned by the student who has this job.

Rigor

The activities in the workstations should range from Depth of Knowledge Level 1 activities to Depth of Knowledge Level 3 and possibly Level 4 questions. Depth of Knowledge (DOK) is a framework designed by Webb (1997) who argues that the cognitive demand of the activity is important.

There are four levels. Level 1 is knowledge/recall. Level 2 requires skill to do the task. Level 3 is strategic thinking; this usually involves some type of explanation about what is being done. Level 4 is usually a long-term project. I saw a great Level 4 activity being done at a school in the south Bronx in a 3rd grade classroom. The teacher had asked the students to design their own question, collect data on it, represent that data in three different types of graphs, and then discuss the shape of the data and which graph was the best representation of that data. This project took the students awhile, but was done very well. It is crucial to think about the different levels of activities that students are engaging in during math workstation time.

One of the things that is stressed when talking about DOK is that it is not about difficulty. Many times, teachers will put difficult tasks in a math workstation but they aren't rigorous. Difficult just means that few people can do it, if any. For example, if I ask *What is a hexagon?* Everyone knows. If I say, *What is a hendecagon?* Hardly anyone knows that off the top of their head. It is a difficult question but not rigorous. It is a Level 1 question that requires recall.

Standards Based

Workstations must be standards based. It is very important to have the standard written on the workstation. It can and probably should be written either as an *I can* statement or *I am learning to* statement, but it must be on the workstation. At any given moment, a student should be able to explain what they are doing and why they are doing it. They need to know what the math is and why they are practicing it. I might even put on the workstation, *This is the math . . .; This is the game to practice the math. . . .*

Location, Location, Location!

Math workstations can be designed to meet the needs of the teacher and the students. I prefer portable stations that can be moved to different work spaces. They can be managed by table leaders. However, other people have static stations that they leave in one place and the students move to those stations during the work period during the transitions. This can also work. I think there is a danger of losing/wasting instruction minutes when students are doing too much moving, but it can work. Some teachers argue that the movement is a good brain break, which is a good reason to have the students move. Some stations are stationary by the very nature of the station. For example, desktops are stationary and so is the interactive board. So, when students are assigned to these workstations, they have to go to them.

Key Points

- Purposeful practice
- First 20 days
- One element of workshop
- Practice makes perfect
- Four must-have workstations
- Flexible groups
- Differentiated/leveled
- Accountability
- Rigor
- Standards
- Portable/fixed

Summary

Math workstations are powerful places (fixed or portable) for students to engage in meaningful practice throughout the year (see Figure 1.7). It is important to start them at the beginning of the year and build a culture of learning together. All stations should be introduced and practiced before they are put into the workstation. The purpose is for students to engage in distributed practice throughout the year on major cluster/priority standard topics. Students must be accountable in the stations for standards-based, academically rigorous, engaging activities.

Figure 1.7

Math Workstations	
Are	**Are not**
Engaging	Boring/worksheets
Interactive	One dimensional
Standards-based	Just fun stuff
Rigorous	All Level 1 activities
Differentiated/leveled	Everyone on the same page at the same time
Require accountability	Free-for-all

Reflection Questions

1. What opportunities do you presently give your students to engage in distributed practice throughout the year?
2. How do you hold yourself accountable for the rigor embedded in the workstation activities?
3. What accountability systems for the work do you presently have set up?
4. What is your biggest takeaway from this chapter? In what ways will it impact your pedagogy?

References

Shannon, Lindsay (2016). Mrs. Shannon's math class website. http://mrsshannonsclass.weebly.com/guided-math.html.

Webb, N. (1997). *Criteria for alignment of expectations and assessments on mathematics and science education*. Washington, DC: National Institute for Science Education.

2

Workstation Management

The first days of school can make or break you. What you do on the first day of school will determine your success or failure for the rest of the year. You will either win or lose your class on the first days of school.

—Wong and Wong (1991, p. 3)

It is said with classroom management that it happens way before the class ever gets there. It's true. You either plan for success or you don't. One of the main parts of doing math workstations is the scheduling. Students need to know where to go, how to get there, and what they should do when they get there. There are many ways to do the schedule. I prefer pictures or colors because they are obvious. Here are some examples of what that could look like (see Figures 2.1, 2.2, and 2.3).

Setting Expectations

Figure 2.1

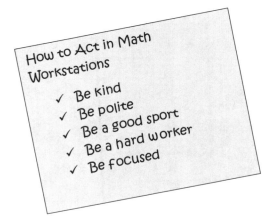

How to Act in Math Workstations
✓ Be kind
✓ Be polite
✓ Be a good sport
✓ Be a hard worker
✓ Be focused

Figure 2.2

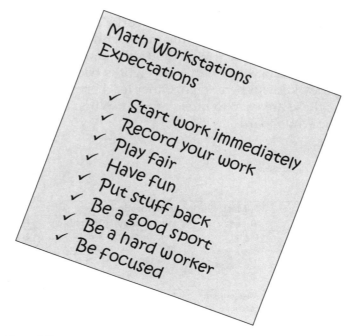

Math Workstations
Expectations

✓ Start work immediately
✓ Record your work
✓ Play fair
✓ Have fun
✓ Put stuff back
✓ Be a good sport
✓ Be a hard worker
✓ Be focused

Figure 2.3

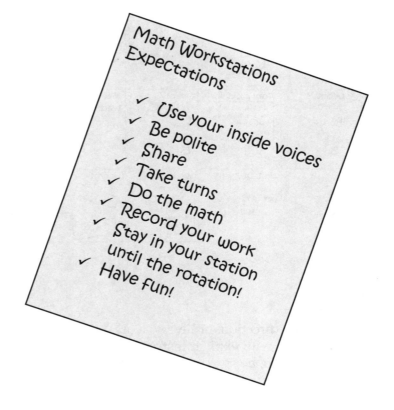

Math Workstations
Expectations

✓ Use your inside voices
✓ Be polite
✓ Share
✓ Take turns
✓ Do the math
✓ Record your work
✓ Stay in your station until the rotation!
✓ Have fun!

Schedules

There are different ways to set up math workstation schedules (see Figures 2.4 and 2.5). Some teachers use students' pictures. I find this works well because then students see themselves and they know exactly where to go. Other teachers use color. I think this also works because the students see the color and they know where to go. Other teachers use Velcro or magnetized pictures; these are easy to move around. While others just write the schedule on the whiteboard.

Figure 2.4

	Monday	Tuesday	Wednesday	Thursday	Friday
Math Workstation Rotation					
Group 1	Meet with the teacher	Digital	Unit: Decimals .87 87 100	Word problems The answer is 10 marbles. What was the division problem?	Fluency 2 × 9 = 18 63 / 9 = 7
Group 2	Fluency 2 × 9 = 18 63 / 9 = 7	Meet with the teacher	Digital	Unit: Decimals .87 87 100	Word problems The answer is 10 marbles. What was the division problem?
Group 3	Word problems The answer is 10 marbles. What was the division problem?	Fluency 2 × 9 = 18 63 / 9 = 7	Meet with the teacher	Digital	Unit: Decimals .87 87 100
Group 4	Unit: Decimals .87 87 100	Word problems The answer is 10 marbles. What was the division problem?	Fluency 2 × 9 = 18 63 / 9 = 7	Meet with the teacher	Digital
Group 5	Digital	Unit: Decimals .87 87 100	Word problems The answer is 10 marbles. Wh at was the division problem?	Fluency 2 × 9 = 18 63 / 9 = 7	Meet with the teacher

Task Cards

It is important to have directions in every workstation (see Figure 2.6). Always have a task card with explicit instructions. It is great to include a step-by step example. Also, be sure to put the *I can* statement on the card. Laminate the workstation direction sheets or put them in sheet protectors to preserve them longer. You could also put QR codes on your task cards so that students can view video examples of the task.

Figure 2.5

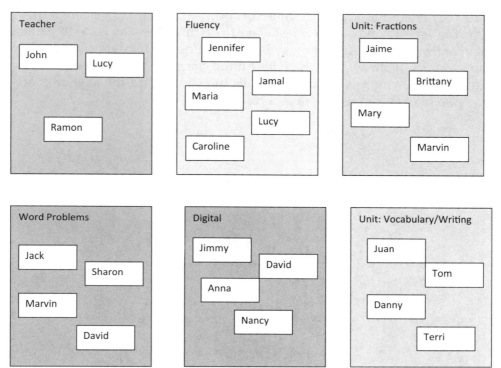

Figure 2.6

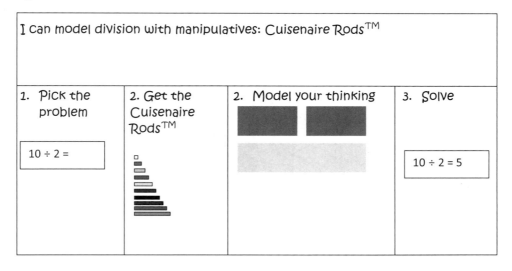

Resources

It is important that students have resources to go to when they get stuck (see Figures 2.7 and 2.8). This is where anchor charts play an important role. All anchor charts from the year should be accessible to the students. Therefore, they should be stored in some sort of way that they are easily retrievable. Binders are one of the easiest ways to do this. One way is to store them all in one big binder. Another way is to have different binders organized by topics/units of study. Put QR codes on the charts so that students can see videos of the concepts/strategies/skills in action. Send the anchor charts home so parents can use them as a resource.

Figure 2.7

Figure 2.8

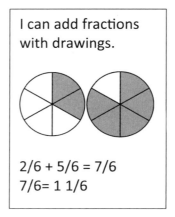

Reflection Sheets

It is important to have students reflect on their daily and weekly activities. Here are some examples of reflection sheets (see Figures 2.9, 2.10, 2.11, and 2.12).

Figure 2.9

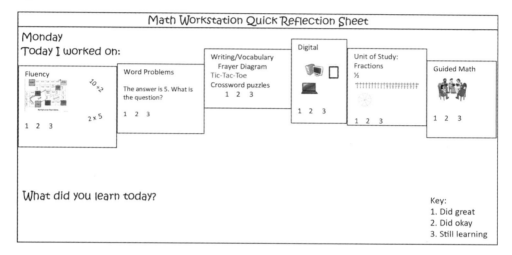

Figure 2.10

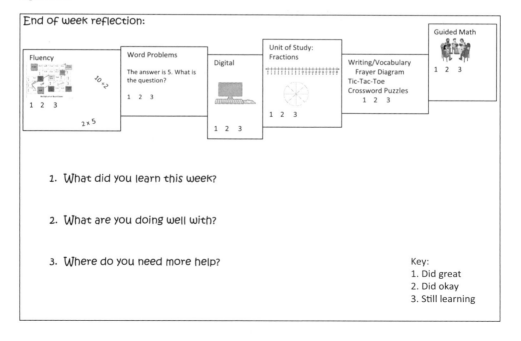

Figure 2.11

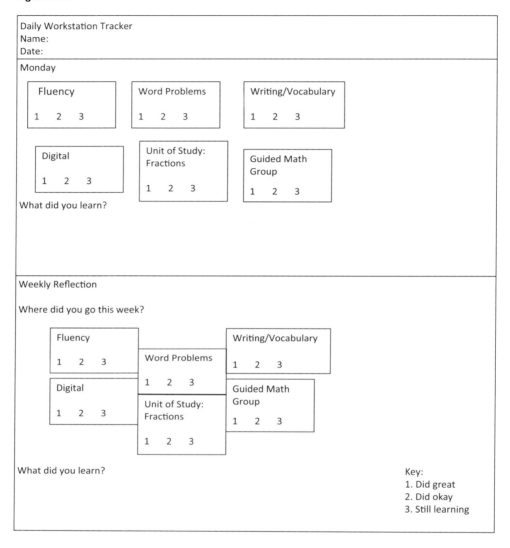

Key Points

- Setting expectations
- Schedules
- Task cards
- Resources
- Reflection sheets

Figure 2.12

```
                        Check Pass for the Week

                      Where have I been this week?

  Fluency        Word Problems      Digital    Vocabulary/Writing    Unit of Study
  ○○               ○○              ○○            ○○                 ○○


  A. What did I learn?



  B. I know it:
  1—Really well   2—Good enough   3—Ok   4—Somewhat   5—Just learning it



  C. What questions do I still have?
```

Summary

Managing math workstations is the key to success. Be sure to spend time setting expectations and modeling out what they look like. It is worth the time investment in the beginning, and it will pay off all year. Make schedules that are student friendly. Get an organization system that works for you and the students. Make sure to practice getting out the workstations and putting them back. The task cards should be self-explanatory and have a QR code when possible. Make sure that students have access to resources that help them *do the math*. Anchor charts can be a great extra teacher's helper in the classroom. Always think about and plan for reflection. It is important that students think about the activities that they did, what they learned well, and what they are still struggling with.

Reflection Questions

1. In what ways do you use your anchor charts as an ongoing conversation throughout the year?

2. How do you communicate practice strategies with parents? What do you think about using QR codes on anchor charts and sending them home?
3. How do you get students to reflect on their work during the week? How often do you keep them accountable: daily, weekly, or in some other way?

Reference

Wong, H. K. and Wong, R. T. (1991). *The first days of school: How to be an effective teacher*. Mountain View, CA: Harry K. Wong Publications, Inc.

Part II

The Four Must-Have Math Workstations

3

Fluency Workstations

Students exhibit computational fluency when they demonstrate flexibility in the computational methods they choose, understand and can explain these methods, and produce accurate answers efficiently.

(NCTM, 2000, p. 152)

Big Ideas (Charles, 2005)

- There is an infinite amount of numbers.
- Numbers can be represented in an infinite amount of equivalent ways.
- We use numbers to represent real-life situations.

Enduring Understandings (Charles, 2005)

- Numbers can be decomposed into parts in an infinite number of ways.
- Adding is the inverse of subtracting.
- Multiplying is the inverse of dividing.
- There are different properties associated with different operations.
- There are many different strategies and models that can be used to perform operations.
- Addition and subtraction are inverse operations.
- Division and multiplication are inverse operations.
- When 0 is divided by any non-zero number the quotient is always zero.

What it Means for a Workstation

The goal of fluency workstations is that students can practice the different operations in their zone of proximal development. It is crucial that we help all students to learn all of the basic facts. That means that some 3rd and 4th graders will be working on automaticity within 20 and some 5th graders will be working on basic multiplication and division facts. Students should practice their facts with a variety of games and activities that foster confidence, competence, and success.

Anchor Charts in Workstations

Throughout the workstations there should be anchor charts that help students to use different strategies and models (see Figures 3.1 and 3.2). In the beginning of the year it is always good to have posters that review basic facts for all operations. As you focus on each operation, build the charts with the students. Review both facts and properties.

Figure 3.1   **Figure 3.2**

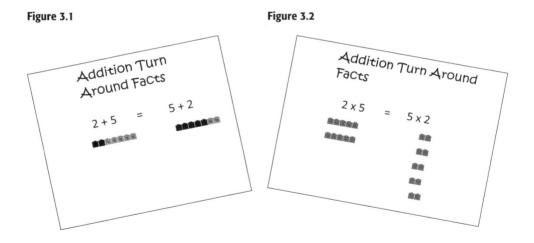

Math Talk Frames

It is important to use talk frames with all students so that they learn how to discuss what they are doing in math. These frames should not only be hung up on anchor charts (about accountable talk) but also put on frames in the workstations to remind students of the types of phraseology that we use when discussing our strategies (see Figures 3.3, 3.4, 3.5, and 3.6).

Figure 3.3

My strategy for solving that is…

Figure 3.4

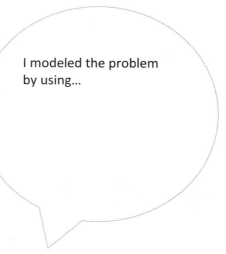

I modeled the problem by using…

Figure 3.5

This is the more efficient strategy because…

Figure 3.6

I solved it using…

Fluency Workstations for Addition

Building Conceptual Understanding of Multi-Digit Addition through Concrete Activities

Concept: There are many different strategies to add multi-digit numbers (see Figures 3.7 and 3.8).
Workstation: Building with base ten blocks.

Figure 3.7

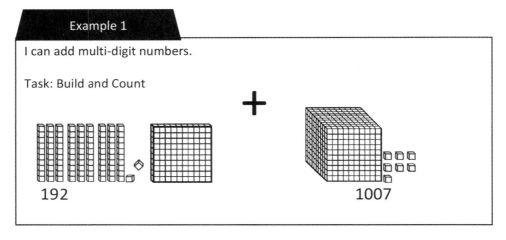

Concept: There are many different strategies to add multi-digit numbers.
Workstation: Building and sketching out multi-digit problems.

Figure 3.8

Example 2

I can add multi-digit numbers.

Task: Add these numbers.   345 + 781 + 296
1. Build it
2. Sketch it
3. Calculate the sum

Building Procedural Fluency and Strategic Competence

Concept: There are many different strategies to add multi-digit numbers (see Figure 3.9). Workstation: Solve in many ways.

Figure 3.9

Example 1

Base Ten Sketch	Place Value	Friendly Numbers Compensation	Traditional Method
523 + 107 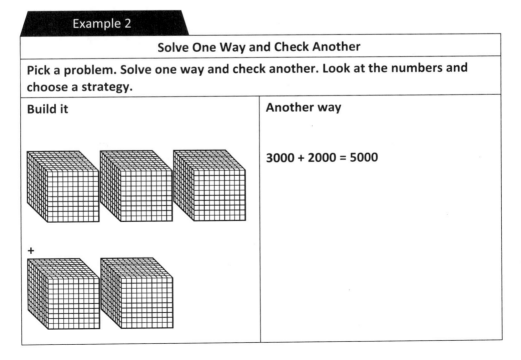	249 + 458 200 + 40 + 9 400 + 50 + 8 600 + 90 + 17 = 707	2599 + 3456 = 2600 + 3455 = 5000 + 1055 = 6055	111 2567 + 3459 6026

Concept: There are many different strategies to add multi-digit numbers. Workstation: Solve in two different ways (see Figures 3.9 and 3.10).

Figure 3.10

Example 2

Solve One Way and Check Another	
Pick a problem. Solve one way and check another. Look at the numbers and choose a strategy.	
Build it	**Another way**
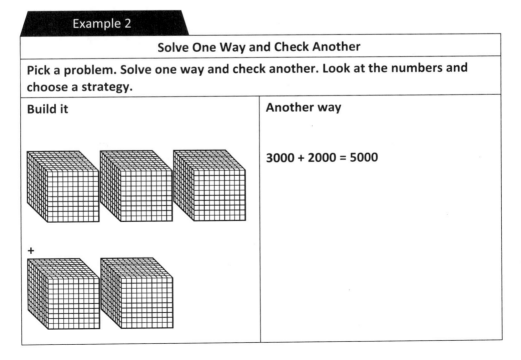	3000 + 2000 = 5000

Building Reasoning Skills

Concept: Reasoning about addition.
Workstation: True or false sorting game (see Figure 3.11).

Figure 3.11

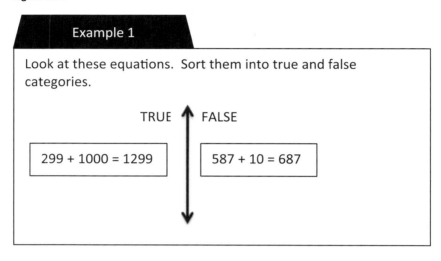

Concept: Sometimes we regroup and sometimes we don't.
Workstation: Regrouping or not? (see Figure 3.12.)

Figure 3.12

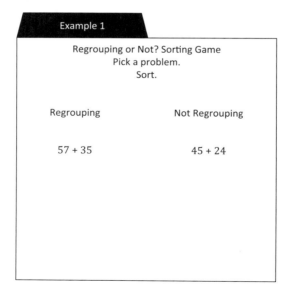

Building Productive Disposition

It is important that students have time to reflect on their learning (see Figures 3.13 and 3.14).

Figure 3.13

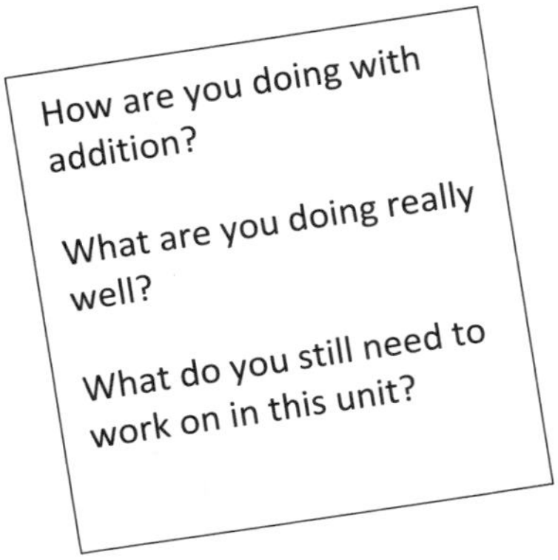

Figure 3.14

How are you doing with addition?

What are you doing really well?

What do you still need to work on in this unit?

Write a one-minute paper about everything you know about addition! Use numbers, words, and pictures.

Fluency Workstations for Subtraction

Building Conceptual Understanding of Multi-Digit Subtraction through Concrete Activities

Concept: There are many different strategies to subtract multi-digit numbers. Workstation: Solving problems with base ten blocks (see Figures 3.15 and 3.16).

Figure 3.15

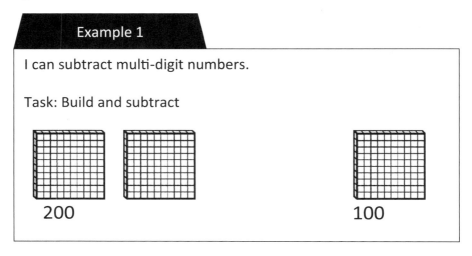

Concept: There are many different strategies to subtract multi-digit numbers. Workstation: Solving problems with base ten blocks and sketches.

Figure 3.16

Example 2

I can subtract multi-digit numbers.

Task: Subtract these numbers. 2000 – 781 =
1. Build it
2. Sketch it
3. Calculate difference

Building Procedural Fluency and Strategic Competence

Concept: There are many different strategies to subtract multi-digit numbers.
Workstation: Solve problem with different strategies (see Figure 3.17).

Figure 3.17

Example 1			
Base Ten Sketch 523 – 107 416	**Place Value (Counting up)** 458 – 289 = 289 + **100** = 389 389 + **11** = 400 400 + **58** = **169**	**Friendly Numbers Compensation** 604 – 478 = 626 – 500 = 126	**Traditional Method** 51 2567 − 459 2108

Concept: There are many different strategies to subtract multi-digit numbers.
Workstation: Solve problem with different strategies (see Figure 3.18).

Figure 3.18

Example 2	
Solve One Way and Check Another	
Pick a problem. Solve one way and check another. Look at the number and choose a strategy.	
Count Up 300 – 258 258 + 42 = 300 42 is the difference	Another Way 300 – 258 = 42

Building Reasoning Skills

Concept: Reasoning about subtraction.
Workstation: True or false sorting game (see Figure 3.19).

Figure 3.19

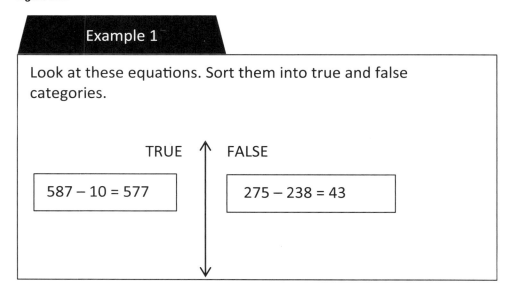

Example 1

Look at these equations. Sort them into true and false categories.

TRUE

587 – 10 = 577

FALSE

275 – 238 = 43

Concept: Addition and subtraction can be used to check (see Figures 3.20 and 3.21).
Workstation: There should be a workstation where students should have to verify their answers by using the inverse operation.

Figure 3.20

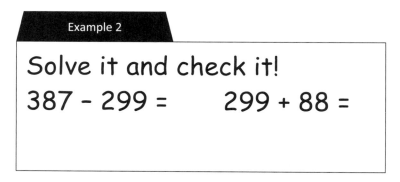

Example 2

Solve it and check it!
387 - 299 =   299 + 88 =

Concept: Sometimes we regroup and sometimes we don't.
Workstation: Regrouping or not?

Figure 3.21

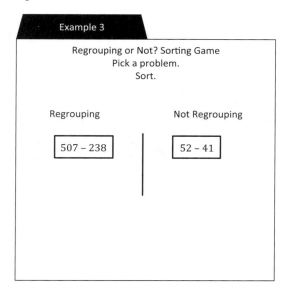

Building Productive Disposition (see Figures 3.22 and 3.23)

Figure 3.22

How are you doing with subtraction?

What are you doing really well?

What do you still need to work on in this unit?

Figure 3.23

Write a one-minute paper about everything you know about subtraction! Use numbers, words, and pictures.

Fluency Workstations for Multiplication

Building Conceptual Understanding through Concrete Activities

Concept: Equal groups.
Workstation: Have the students group sets of pony beads together to represent the different multiplication tables (see Figures 3.24 and 3.25).

Figure 3.24

Concept: Equal groups.
Workstation: Have the students choose a fact to build with base ten blocks.

Figure 3.25

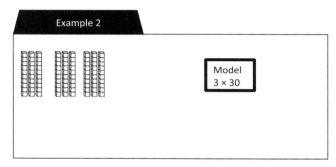

Building Conceptual Understanding through Pictorial Activities

Concept: Equal groups.
Workstation: Have the students choose a fact to build with base ten blocks (see Figure 3.26).

Figure 3.26

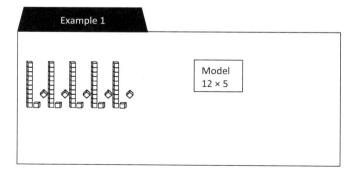

Concept: Equal groups (see Figure 3.27).
Workstation: Students get two dice—one for how many circles and the other for how many stars in each. Students draw it, write the repeated addition sentence, write the groups of verbal statement, and then write the multiplication statement.

Figure 3.27

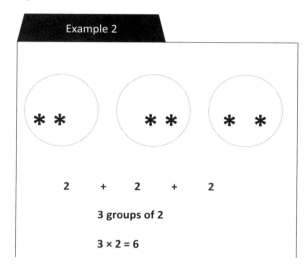

Concept: Arrays (see Figure 3.28).
Workstation: Students get two dice—one is for the rows and the other is for the columns. The students circle the intersections and then determine the product.

Figure 3.28

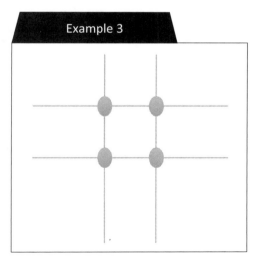

Concept: Visual representation of multi-digit multiplication (see Figures 3.29 and 3.30).
Workstation: Students choose an expression and represent it with a mathematical sketch/drawing or diagram.

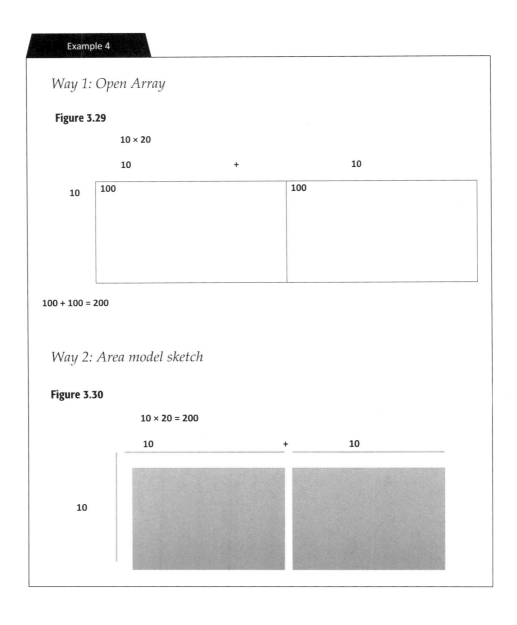

Example 4

Way 1: Open Array

Figure 3.29

10 × 20

10 + 10

10 | 100 | 100

100 + 100 = 200

Way 2: Area model sketch

Figure 3.30

10 × 20 = 200

10 + 10

10

Building Conceptual Understanding through Abstract Activities

Concept: Multiplication properties (commutative, associative, distributive). Workstation: This is a match/concentration game. Students have to match all the cards that go with the expression. Students can play this game competitively, by turning all the cards face down and then turning them over looking for the matches. They can also play this game collaboratively, working together with the cards turned face up and trying to get all the matches done. (See Figure 3.31.)

Figure 3.31

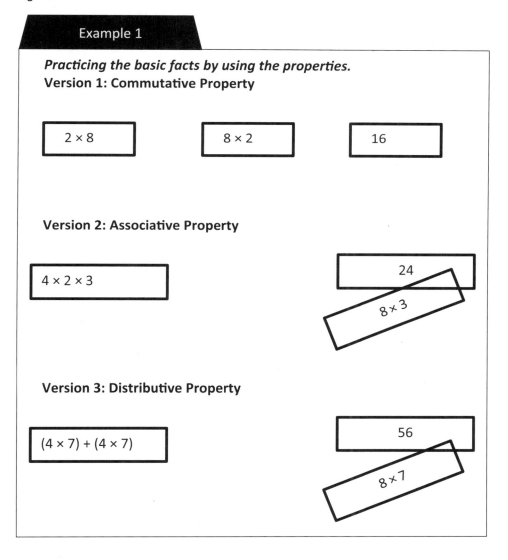

Example 1

Practicing the basic facts by using the properties.
Version 1: Commutative Property

| 2 × 8 | | 8 × 2 | | 16 |

Version 2: Associative Property

4 × 2 × 3

24

8 × 3

Version 3: Distributive Property

(4 × 7) + (4 × 7)

56

8 × 7

Concept: Efficient strategies depend on the numbers (see Figures 3.32 and 3.33). Workstation: Have the students sort which strategies they would use with which facts and then explain why.

Figure 3.32

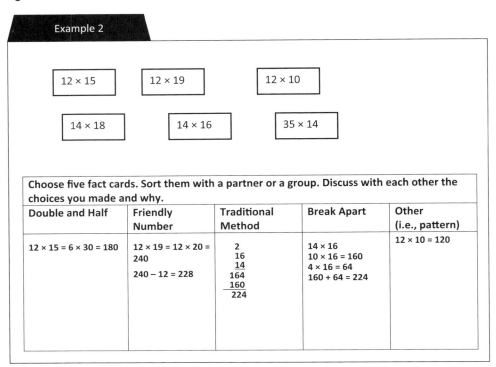

Example 2

| 12 × 15 | 12 × 19 | 12 × 10 |

| 14 × 18 | 14 × 16 | 35 × 14 |

Choose five fact cards. Sort them with a partner or a group. Discuss with each other the choices you made and why.

Double and Half	Friendly Number	Traditional Method	Break Apart	Other (i.e., pattern)
12 × 15 = 6 × 30 = 180	12 × 19 = 12 × 20 = 240 240 − 12 = 228	2 16 14 164 160 224	14 × 16 10 × 16 = 160 4 × 16 = 64 160 + 64 = 224	12 × 10 = 120

Figure 3.33

Example 3

Choose a multiplication fact. Solve one way and check another.

Solve One Way	Check Another
15 × 18 10 × 18 = 180 5 × 18 = 90 180 + 90 = 270	15 × 18 120 + 150 270

Building Reasoning Skills

Concept: Reasoning about multiplication.
Workstation: True or false sorting game (see Figure 3.34).

Figure 3.34

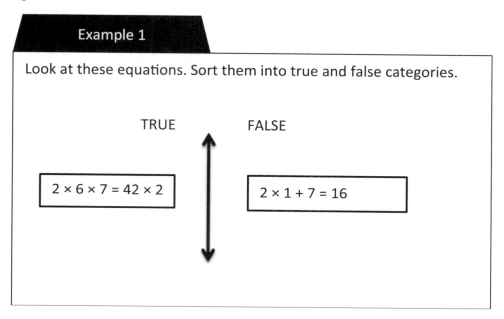

Example 1

Look at these equations. Sort them into true and false categories.

TRUE   FALSE

$2 \times 6 \times 7 = 42 \times 2$ $2 \times 1 + 7 = 16$

Concept: Equality (see Figure 3.35).
Workstation: What's missing?

Figure 3.35

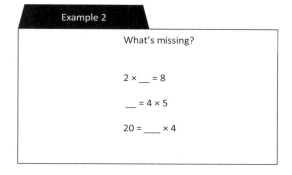

Example 2

What's missing?

$2 \times \_\_ = 8$

$\_\_ = 4 \times 5$

$20 = \_\_ \times 4$

Building a Productive Disposition

Students should be given the opportunity to reflect on their learning throughout the unit of study (see Figures 3.36 and 3.37).

Figure 3.36

How are you doing with multiplication?

What are you doing really well?

What do you still need to work on in this unit?

Figure 3.37

Write a one-minute paper about everything you know about multiplication! Use numbers, words, and pictures.

Fluency Workstations for Division

Building Conceptual Understanding through Concrete Activities

Concept: Understanding division (see Figure 3.38).
Workstation: Have students use Cuisenaire Rods™ to model division.

Figure 3.38

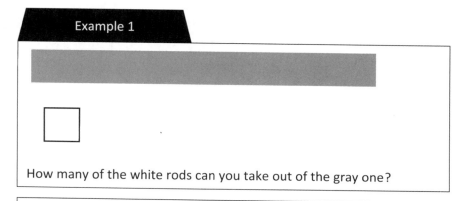

Example 1

How many of the white rods can you take out of the gray one?

$$8 \div 1 = 8$$
You can take 8 1s out of 8.

Concept: Understanding division (see Figure 3.39).
Workstation: Have students model division with counters.

Figure 3.39

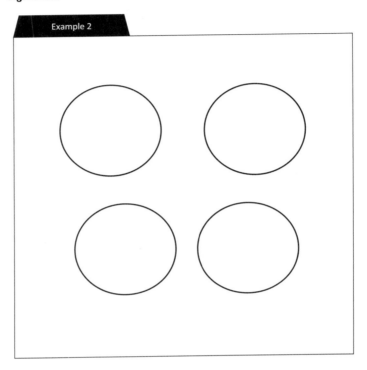

On the front:

You are dividing by 4. Take 4 counters. Divide them among the 4 circles. How many are there?

On the back:

$$4 \div 4 = 1$$

Concept: Understanding division (see Figure 3.40).
Workstation: Have students model division with counters.

Figure 3.40

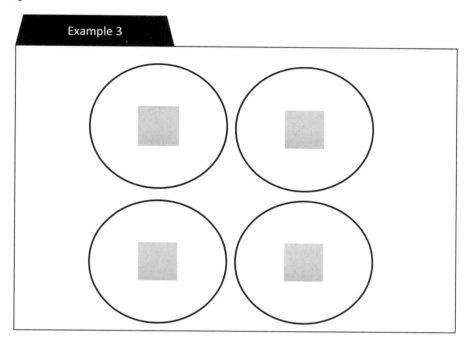

Write a story to go with the picture:

Mom shared 4 cookies with 4 boys.
How many cookies did each boy get?

Concept: Understanding division (see Figure 3.41).
Workstation: Have students model division with counters.

Figure 3.41

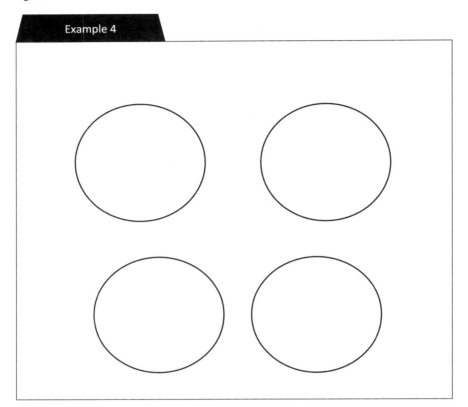

On the front:

Act out this problem on the story mat. There are 4 friends and 5 cookies.
How many cookies does each friend get? Are there any left over? If so,
how many?

On the back:

5 ÷ 4 = 1 with a
remainder of 1
Each friend gets 1 cookie and there is 1 cookie left over.

Concept: Understanding remainders (see Figure 3.42).
Workstation: Have students use a visual model to solve remainder problems.

Figure 3.42

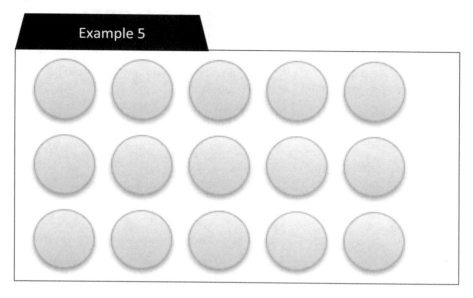

Look at the array. If there are 2 friends that are going to share these 15 gum balls, how many will each friend get? Are there any left over? If so, how many?

Each friend will get 7 pieces. There will be 1 left over.

$$15 \div 2 = 7 \ r1$$

Concept: Understanding division (see Figures 3.43 and 3.44).
Workstation: Have students use drawings and diagrams to model division.

Figure 3.43

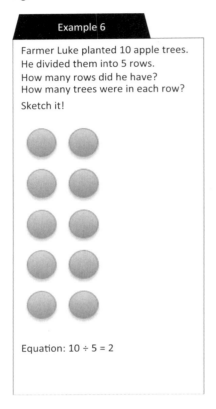

Example 6

Farmer Luke planted 10 apple trees.
He divided them into 5 rows.
How many rows did he have?
How many trees were in each row?

Sketch it!

Equation: 10 ÷ 5 = 2

Figure 3.44

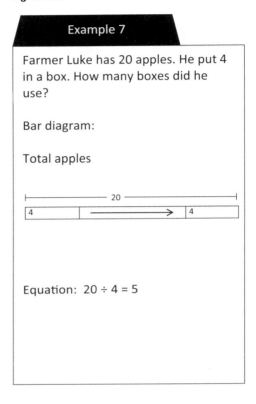

Example 7

Farmer Luke has 20 apples. He put 4 in a box. How many boxes did he use?

Bar diagram:

Total apples

Equation: 20 ÷ 4 = 5

Concept: There are different types of division problems—equal groups, arrays, and comparison problems (see Figure 3.45).
Workstation: Categorize and solve division problems.

Figure 3.45

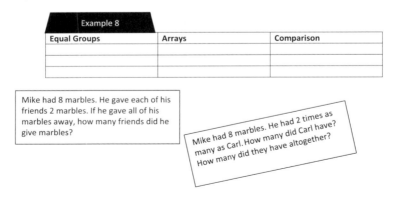

Example 8

Equal Groups	Arrays	Comparison

Mike had 8 marbles. He gave each of his friends 2 marbles. If he gave all of his marbles away, how many friends did he give marbles?

Mike had 8 marbles. He had 2 times as many as Carl. How many did Carl have? How many did they have altogether?

Building Procedural Fluency

Concept: Division quotients can be found by thinking about the related multiplication fact (see Figure 3.46).
Workstation: There should be a workstation where students have to match the related multiplication and division facts. Use the expressions rather than equations in this game because otherwise some students will just look to match numbers. This activity should require students to think.

Figure 3.46

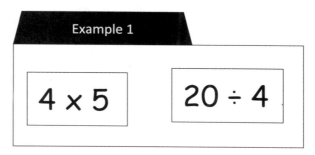

Concept: Multiplication can be used to check division (see Figure 3.47).
Workstation: There should be a workstation where students should have to verify their answers by using multiplication.

Figure 3.47

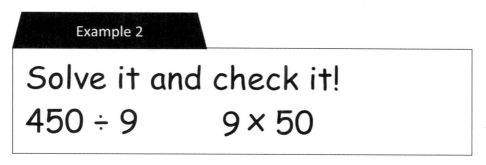

Building Strategic Competence

Concept: Modeling basic division facts (see Figure 3.48).
Workstation: Students represent different division facts.

Figure 3.48

Example 1	
Write your fact: 4/2	
Repeated Subtraction $4 - 2 = 2$ $2 - 2 = 0$	**Array**
Bar Diagram **4 total** | 2	2
---|---|	**Equal Group**
Word Problem *Sue had 4 cookies. She split them equally with her brother. How many did each person get?* **Answer:** **Check with multiplication: $2 \times 2 = 4$**	

Concept: Break apart big numbers to make calculations into simpler ones.
Workstation: Solve one way and check another (see Figures 3.49 and 3.50).

Figure 3.49

Example 2

Solve using area model.
Build it. Sketch it. Show it with numbers.
Double Digit by Single Digit
Double Digit by Double Digit
Triple Digit by Double Digit

137/11

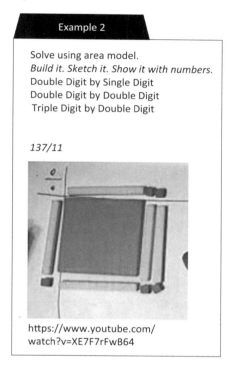

https://www.youtube.com/
watch?v=XE7F7rFwB64

Figure 3.50

Example 3

Solve using an array.
Build it. Sketch it. Show it with numbers.
Double Digit by Single Digit
Double Digit by Double Digit
Triple Digit by Double Digit

137/ 11

10	+ 1	+ 1	
110	11	11	REMAINDER 5

Concept: Break apart big numbers to make calculations into simpler ones.
Workstation: Solve one way and check another (see Figure 3.51).

Figure 3.51

Example 4	
Solve One Way and Check Another	
Pick a problem. Solve one way and check another. Look at the number and choose a strategy.	
One Way	**Another Way**
460 ÷ 8 400 ÷ 8 = 50 60 ÷ 8 = 7 with remainder of 4 57 r4	**8 × 50 = 400** **8 × 7 = 56** **4 more makes 60** **so quotient is 57 r4**

Building Reasoning Skills

Concept: Reasoning about division.
Workstation: True or false sorting game (see Figure 3.52).

Figure 3.52

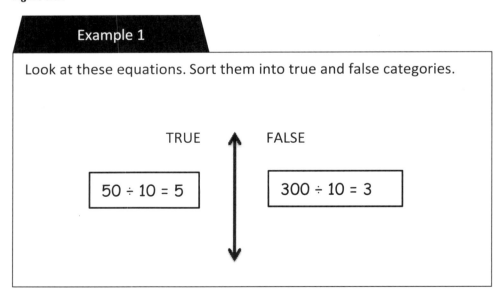

Example 1

Look at these equations. Sort them into true and false categories.

TRUE ⬍ FALSE

50 ÷ 10 = 5   300 ÷ 10 = 3

Concept: Reasoning about division.
Workstation: What does not belong? (See Figure 3.53.)

Figure 3.53

Example 2

What does not belong? Why?

50 ÷ 10   15 ÷ 3   500 ÷ 100   72 ÷ 9

60 ÷ 12

Concept: Reasoning about remainders (see Figure 3.54).
Workstation: What happens to this remainder?

Figure 3.54

Example 3

Figuring out remainders:
Pick a problem.
Record it. Solve it. Write the remainder. Interpret it!

Problems	Model	Remainder	Round Up/Down/Drop/Leave
The 3rd graders are going on a field trip. There are 67 students and 5 adults. Each mini-van fits 15 people. How many mini vans do they need?	72/15 72/15 = 4 r12	12	In this case we have to round up. We need 5 buses because the 12 people have to have a place to sit.

Concept: Remainders depend upon the context (see Figure 3.55).
Workstation: What happens to this remainder?

Figure 3.55

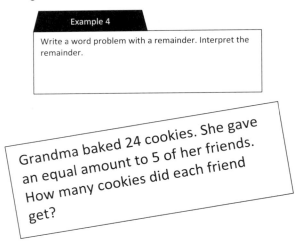

Example 4

Write a word problem with a remainder. Interpret the remainder.

Grandma baked 24 cookies. She gave an equal amount to 5 of her friends. How many cookies did each friend get?

Concept: Sometimes there are remainders/the remainder must be less than the divisor (see Figure 3.56).
Workstation: Remainder or not?

Figure 3.56

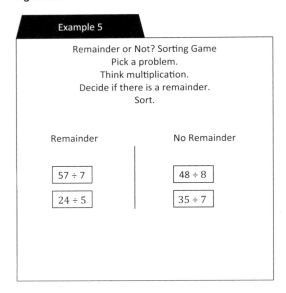

Example 5

Remainder or Not? Sorting Game
Pick a problem.
Think multiplication.
Decide if there is a remainder.
Sort.

Remainder   No Remainder

57 ÷ 7   48 ÷ 8

24 ÷ 5   35 ÷ 7

Building Productive Disposition (See Figures 3.57 and 3.58)

Figure 3.57

How are you doing with division?

What are you doing really well?

What do you still need to work on in this unit?

Figure 3.58

Write a one-minute paper about everything you know about division! Use numbers, words, and pictures.

Culminating Activities

At the end of the unit there are different learning structures to help students review and show their understanding of the concepts. Here is an example of what this might look like at the end of a multiplication unit (see Figures 3.59, 3.60, 3.61, and 3.62).

Choice Boards

It is important to give students choice boards so that they can choose ways to demonstrate their learning of the content. In this particular board, the students have to choose three things, make a plan with some deadlines, and follow the rubrics to complete the plan.

Figure 3.59

Choice Board		
You must choose two things from the board to do by the end of the unit. You can work on these projects in your workstations and at home. Please submit your plan to Ms. Thomas by next Wednesday, February 18th. Be sure to look at the specific rubric for your projects.		
Make a poster about multiplication.	Make a Glog about multiplication.	Design your own project about multiplication.
Make a board game to practice multiplication strategies.	Write an essay about different multiplication strategies. Use numbers, words, and pictures.	Make a PowerPoint about multiplication.
Do the Find Someone Who Can board.	Make a card game to practice multiplication strategies.	Make a podcast about multiplication.

Figure 3.60

My Plan for the Multiplication Projects

Week 1:
First, I will work on the poster project. I am going to do this by myself. I will do this in the Vocabulary/Writing workstation.

Week 2:
Then I will work on a strategy board game. I will also do this in the Fluency workstation. I am going to design the game in a group.

Find Someone Who is more like a group review where several people are involved and everybody is learning.

Figure 3.61

MULTIPLICATION: FIND SOMEONE WHO…		
I understand multi-digit multiplication strategies. I can discuss and explain different strategies. Task: During project choice time take the board and find different people to fill in your board. Each person must sign their name and prove that they can do the task. They can either write it on the board or on another piece of paper. Each person can only answer one time.		
Multiply using the area model. Signature:	Multiply using the open array. Signature:	Multiply using compensation (friendly numbers). Signature:
Multiply using place value strategies. Signature:	Multiply using the traditional method. Signature:	Solve one way and check another. Signature:
Solve 299 × 4 using mental math. Signature:	Multiply using partial products. Signature:	Explain and give an example of doubling and halving. Signature:

True or false sorts allow the students to reason about the learned concepts. These tend to be tricky for students and require that they stop, concentrate, and then make thinking decisions before they choose an answer.

Figure 3.62

True or False Sort

I can sort place value statements.

Task: Pick a card. Decide whether or not it is true or false. Sort the facts. Turn them over and verify if you are correct or not.

92 = (9 × 10) + (2 × 1)

3272 > (3 × 1000) + (7 × 10) + (2 × 100) + (2 × 1)

True	False

Teaching in the 21st Century

There is a plethora of tools that students can use to develop math fluency. Be sure to read the books and do some of the activities in the books. Be sure to download the paper manipulatives, hundreds grids, thousands grids, ten thousands grids, number lines, and more. Have the students play some of the internet games as well (see Figure 3.63).

Figure 3.63

Picture Books	Videos	Virtual Tools	Internet Games
One is a Snail, Ten is a Crab by April Pulley Sayre & Jeff Sayre	Learnzillion.com	https://www.mathlearningcenter.org/resources/apps	http://www.multiplication.com/games/all-games
512 Ants on Sullivan Street by Carol Losi			http://www.mathplayground.com/games.html
If You Were a Multiplication Sign by Trisha Speed Shaskan			http://jmathpage.com/topics/jmpfronttopics.html
If You Were a Division Sign by Trisha Speed Shaskan			http://www.math-play.com/
Panda Math by Ann Nagda			
Cheetah Math by Ann Nagda			
Multiplying Menace by Pam Calvert			
Amanda Bean's Amazing Dream by Cindy Neuschwander			
One Grain of Rice by Demi			
The Best of Times by Greg Tang			

Key Points

Cycle of engagement:

* Concrete
* Pictorial
* Abstract

Summary

Fluency is really important and students need a great deal of opportunities to practice it throughout the year. There should be activities ranging from single digit to multi-digit operations. Students should be able to work with concrete materials as well as draw out/sketch math models. Strategy is key. Students have to be able to look at the structure of numbers in a variety of ways and think about efficient ways to operate on those numbers accordingly. The fluency station stays up all year long and students work in their zone of proximal development, always working toward grade level goals.

Reflection Questions

1. What do you currently do in your fluency workstation?
2. Do you have a variety of opportunities for students to practice different strategies?
3. What new ideas do you have from this chapter?
4. What is one change that you will make?

References

Charles, R. (2005). Big ideas and understandings as the foundation for elementary and middle school mathematics. *NCSM Journal of Mathematics Education Leadership*, 7(3).

National Council of Teachers of Mathematics. (2000). *Principles and standards for school mathematics*. Reston, VA: National Council of Teachers of Mathematics.

4

The Word Problem Workstation

> It is better to solve one problem five ways than to solve five problems one way.
>
> (Pólya, 1957)

Big Ideas

There are several different categories of word problems. These categories can be arranged into a hierarchy.

Enduring Understandings

- There are addition, subtraction, multiplication, division, and compare problems.
- The key word strategy should not be used.
- Models are important.
- There are a variety of models (i.e., pattern blocks, counters, drawings, tables, tape diagrams).
- It is important to make a plan, do a model, and double check the work.

What it Means for a Workstation

Word problems are notoriously difficult for students. Therefore, besides having a problem of the day routine, teachers should have a word problem workstation. The goal of the word problem workstation is that students have the opportunity to practice word problems in their zone of proximal development. This station should have a variety of activities. The problems should be differentiated based on the children's ability to solve problems in the hierarchy. Meaning that students should not be working on a Level 8 problem if they cannot solve a Level 2 problem. These problem types never change. The numbers we use in them change (whole numbers, fractions, decimals, etc.), but the problem types never change. The idea is that students do not rely on a key word strategy but rather that they understand the problem type or more specifically what the problem is asking them to solve.

There is a hierarchy to word problems, and it is important to assess and find out if there are any gaps in students' understanding and then to plan for those in the workstation. The different activities that students engage in should be differentiated. Therefore, everybody should not be doing the same problems at the same time.

There should be a variety of opportunities for working with, modeling, and strategizing about word problems. Students should solve word problems, write word problems, sort word problems, and match word problems with models, strategies, and solutions. Students should do these activities alone, with partners, and in groups. All students should have their own problem-solving folder.

Anchor Charts in the Workstation

There should be anchor charts that talk about the practice/process of solving word problems. There should also be charts about the types of word problems (see Figures 4.1, 4.2, 4.3, 4.4, and 4.5) (see Carpenter, Fennema, Franke, Levi, and Empson, 2014).

Figure 4.1

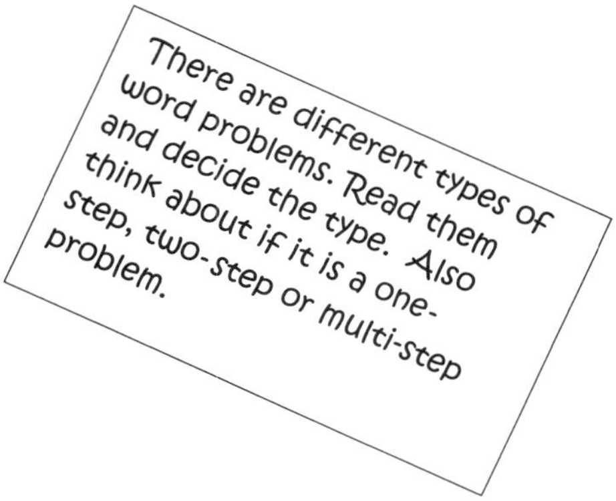

There are different types of word problems. Read them and decide the type. Also think about if it is a one-step, two-step or multi-step problem.

Figure 4.2

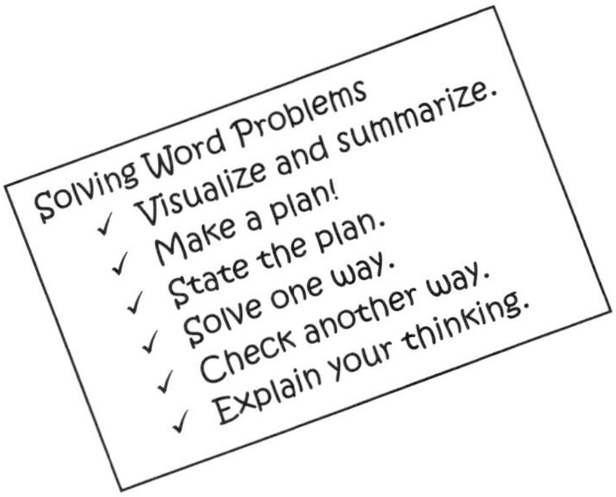

Solving Word Problems
✓ Visualize and summarize.
✓ Make a plan!
✓ State the plan.
✓ Solve one way.
✓ Check another way.
✓ Explain your thinking.

Math Talk Frames

Figure 4.3

This is a _____ type of problem.

Figure 4.4

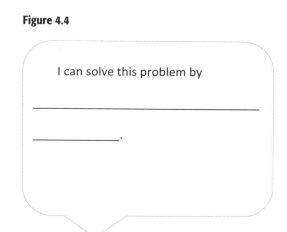

I can solve this problem by _____

_____.

Figure 4.5

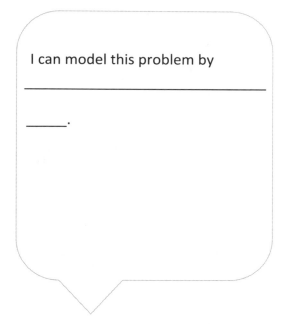

I can model this problem by _____

_____.

The Types of Problems

L represents the level of the problem.

Figure 4.6

	Add to Result Unknown	Change Unknown	Start Unknown
Join	There were 59 students in the cafeteria. If 67 more students came, how many are there now? L1	There were 59 students in the cafeteria. Some more students came. Now there are 126 students in the cafeteria. How many came? L6	There were some students in the cafeteria. 67 more students came. Now there are 100 students in the cafeteria. How many were there in the beginning? L14
Separate	There was a whole pan of brownies on the table. The students ate 2/6 of the brownies. How much is left? L2	There was a whole pan of brownies on the table. The students ate some. Now there is 4/6 of the pan left. How much did they eat? L7	There were some brownies on the table. The students ate 2/6 of the brownies. Now there is 4/6 of the brownies left. How much of the pan of brownies was on the table in the beginning? L15
	Whole Unknown	**Part Unknown**	**Both Addends Unknown**
Part-Part Whole	The bakery had 125 lemon cupcakes and 189 strawberry cupcakes. How many cupcakes did they have altogether? L3	The bakery had 125 lemon cupcakes. They had some strawberry cupcakes. Altogether they had 314 cupcakes. How many strawberry cupcakes did they have? L5	The bakery had 10 cupcakes. Some were chocolate and some were vanilla. How many of each could it have had? L4
Compare	**Difference Unknown**	**Bigger Part Unknown**	**Smaller Part Unknown**
	Tom had 57 marbles. Clay had 68. How many more marbles did Clay have than Tom? How many did they have altogether? L8	Tom had 57 marbles. Clay had 11 more marbles than Tom. How many marbles did Clay have? How many marbles did they have altogether? L10	Clay had 68 marbles. Tom had 11 fewer marbles than he did. How many did Tom have? How many did they have altogether? L11
	Tom had 57 marbles. Clay had 68. How many fewer marbles did Tom have than Clay? L9	Tom had 57 marbles. He had 11 fewer than Clay. How many did Clay have? L12	Clay had 68 marbles. He had 11 more than Tom. How many did Tom have? L13

It is important to give students a word problem test at the beginning of the year and then a few times throughout to see where they are on the problem-solving hierarchy. Multi-step word problems are just problems with more than one type in the problem. With this information, teachers can plan accordingly. If students can't solve an *add to start unknown problem*, then they shouldn't be working on a multi-step, two operation problem. See Figures 4.6 and 4.7 for examples.

Figure 4.7

	Multiplication	Division (How many in each group?)	Division (How many groups?)
Equal Groups	There are 5 baskets with 20 apples in each. How many apples are there altogether? L1	There were 10 apples. There were 5 boxes. The apples were shared equally into the boxes. How many apples were in each box? L3	There were 10 apples. The farmer put 2 in a box. How many boxes did he use? L5
Array	There are 15 rows of apple trees with 10 trees in each row. How many trees are there altogether? L2	There were 100 trees. There were planted equally in 10 rows. How many were in each row? L4	There were 100 trees. The farmer planted 10 in each row. How many rows did he have? L6
	Difference Unknown	Smaller Part Unknown	Bigger Part Unknown
Compare	Ray had 9 marbles. Don had 2 times as many as he did. How many did Don have? L7	Don had 18 marbles. He had 2 times as many as Ray. How many did Ray have? L8	Don had 18 marbles. Ray had 9 marbles. How many times as many marbles did Don have as Ray? L9

Beyond Answer Getting

The other important thing about the problem-solving center is that the goal should be more than "answer getting." The goal is to teach students how to engage in the problem-solving process. We want them to visualize and summarize the problem, make a plan to solve the problem, and then double-double check their work (meaning to check the math and to check to see if the answer makes sense). Sometimes students will do the math correctly but they will have used the wrong operation. Checklists help students to self-monitor (see Figure 4.8).

Example of a Checklist

Figure 4.8

Math Word Problem Checklist			
	Self	Peer	Teacher
Read the problem twice.			
Visualize the problem.			
Write a set-up equation.			
Make a plan.			
Do the math.			
Check a different way.			
Write an equation to show the math.			
Write the answer with the units.			
Explain how you solved the problem.			

Cycle of Engagement

When teaching students to solve word problems it is important to teach them through the cycle of engagement. First, teach students to model problems with different manipulatives. Next, teach them to draw out their thinking with sketches. Finally, teach them how to make sense of it all with the numbers. We tend to rush through the cycle to get to the abstract level way before the students have a conceptual understanding of what they are doing. In a workstation, there should be storytelling mats where students have to solve with the manipulatives (see Figure 4.9).

Example Word Problem Workstations

Concept: Solving problems with concrete objects.
Workstation: Using snap cubes to solve problems.

Figure 4.9

Snap cubes/One-inch tiles

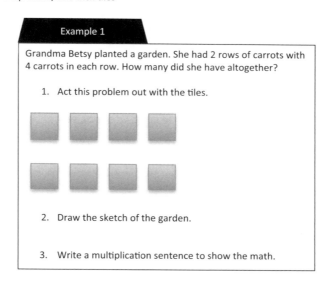

Example 1

Grandma Betsy planted a garden. She had 2 rows of carrots with 4 carrots in each row. How many did she have altogether?

1. Act this problem out with the tiles.

2. Draw the sketch of the garden.

3. Write a multiplication sentence to show the math.

Rekenrek

This is a tool from the Freundenthal Institute in Holland. It is gaining popularity in the US, mostly for use with primary students doing addition and subtraction. I find it is fabulous for doing many types of word problems. Here is an example (see Figure 4.10).

Concept: Solving problems with tools.
Workstation: Using the rekenrek to solve problems.

Figure 4.10

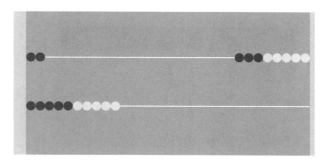

Figure 4.11

Miguel has 2 marbles. Carlos has 5 times as many as he does. How many does Carlos have?

1. Solve on your rekenrek.

2. Draw a sketch of how it looks.

3. Now turn your sketch into a tape diagram.

4. Show how you can solve this problem with numbers.

Cuisenaire Rods™

(Bring them back . . . search the basements and closets.)

Cuisenaire Rods™ are the forgotten manipulative. They are great to teach basic operations as well as fractions. Every school has them hidden somewhere deep in a closet because they used to be as ubiquitous as teddy bears are today (see Figure 4.12).

Concept: Solving problems with tools.
Workstation: Using the Cuisenaire Rods™ to solve problems.

Figure 4.12

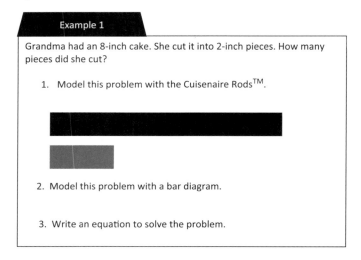

Example 1

Grandma had an 8-inch cake. She cut it into 2-inch pieces. How many pieces did she cut?

1. Model this problem with the Cuisenaire Rods™.

2. Model this problem with a bar diagram.

3. Write an equation to solve the problem.

Tape Diagram/Strip Diagram

Using tape diagrams (strip diagrams/bar models) is an important tool for solving word problems. Almost all state standards now require that students know how to do this. From the example above, you can see how easy it is to go from modeling with Cuisenaire Rods™ to being able to draw a tape diagram.

These diagrams help students to unpack word problems (see Figure 4.13). They have been in the literature on word problems for years. Fortunately, today there are some digital resources to also help scaffold our understanding about how to do this. One such site is called Math Playground: Thinking Block Videos. This is a great site. They have several videos that teach tape diagramming. They also have a different part of the site where teachers can pull up word problems or make up their own, and have the students come up to the interactive board and use the tools on the screen to solve problems with tape diagrams. They also have an independent section where students can go in and track their work. It is free, iPad friendly (as well as laptop friendly), and really educational. Greg Tang has also posted a Word Problem Generator that generates different types of word problems and then scaffolds student thinking by giving them a hint of how to set up the tape diagram.

See http://www.mathplayground.com/thinkingblocks.html and http://gregtangmath.com/materials.

Concept: Solving problems with strip/tape diagrams.
Workstation: Using the strip/tape diagrams to solve problems.

Figure 4.13

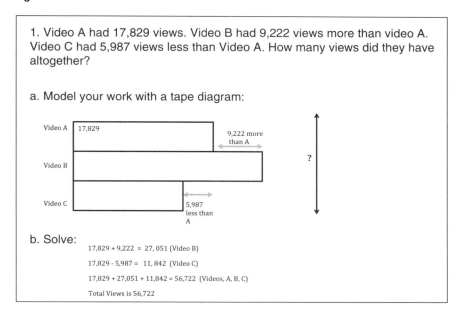

1. Video A had 17,829 views. Video B had 9,222 views more than video A. Video C had 5,987 views less than Video A. How many views did they have altogether?

a. Model your work with a tape diagram:

Video A | 17,829 | 9,222 more than A
Video B
Video C | 5,987 less than A | ?

b. Solve:

17,829 + 9,222 = 27,051 (Video B)

17,829 - 5,987 = 11,842 (Video C)

17,829 + 27,051 + 11,842 = 56,722 (Videos, A, B, C)

Total Views is 56,722

More Models

It is important to have opportunities for students to model their thinking throughout the year. Be sure to use counters, number lines, one-inch tiles, fraction manipulatives, as well as decimal manipulatives. Many of these manipulatives should be in their toolkits (see Figures 4.14, 4.15, 4.16, 4.17, and 4.18).

Figure 4.14

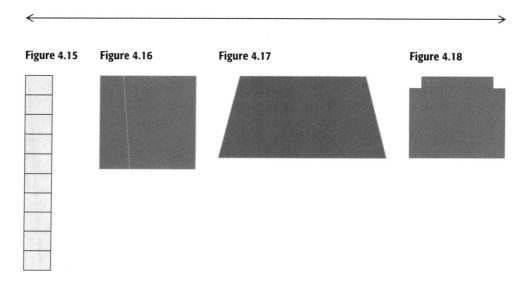

Figure 4.15   **Figure 4.16**   **Figure 4.17**   **Figure 4.18**

Decontextualizing

Decontextualizing is what we usually do with word problems. We give students the problems and they have to find the answer. There are many ways to scaffold these types of problems. One way is to use templates. Templates are a navigation tool for students. They help them to find their way. They lay out a clear path. They can be either a basic framework or extremely detailed. Templates are simply scaffolds and eventually they are faded out so that students can do the work independently (see Figures 4.19 and 4.20).

Concept: Solving problems with templates
Workstation: Using the templates to solve problems

Figure 4.19

Example 1	
Word Problem Template	
What type of word problem is this? Addition Subtraction Multiplication Division One-step Multi-step	Make a picture in your head. Write an equation that shows what you are looking for?
Now, what's your plan to solve the problem?	Check your plan a different way.
Write the answer.	Explain your thinking.

Figure 4.20

Example 2	
Word Problem Template	
Read the problem twice. Visualize the problem. What is it about?	What is your plan?
Solve the problem one way.	Check your plan a different way.
Write the answer.	Explain your thinking.

Contextualizing

It is equally important to have problems where students have to contextualize. This means where students see numbers and have to think about them and make up contexts where these numbers make sense (see Figure 4.21).

Concept: Students should write their own problems.
Workstation: Writing word problems.

Figure 4.21

Example 1

The answer is 12 marbles. What is the question?
(It was a division problem)

Write your problem:

Model your problem:

Write the equation:

Two Argument Problems

Two argument problems are problems where students have to reason about the answer to decide which argument makes the most sense (see Figure 4.22).

Concept: Reasoning about the logic of others.
Workstation: Students have to read, reason about, and discuss the thinking of others.

Figure 4.22

Example 1
Example of a Two-Argument Problem
Problem: May said that 1/8 is larger than 1/4 because 8 is bigger than 4. Kate disagreed because she said that a 1/4 is a larger piece of a pie than 1/8 if the pies are the same size. Who is correct?

Think about the arguments. *Who do think is correct?*	**Decide and defend your thinking.** *Why did you think this?*
Prove your thinking with a model.	**Prove your thinking with numbers.**

In the bag with this problem would be a series of tools to scaffold student thinking such as pattern blocks, fraction circles, and bars and number lines. Students should be able to use these tools to reason about the numbers in the problem. They should be able to explain their thinking as well.

Find and Fix the Error

In these problems the students are trying to find and fix an error in the solution of a word problem (see Figure 4.23). These errors are common errors that students make, what Ginsburg (1987) calls "bugs." The more time that students get to talk with each other about problems and reason out loud by modeling their thinking, the clearer they can get about the problem.

Concept: Reasoning about the logic of others.
Workstation: Students have to read, reason about, and discuss the thinking of others.

Figure 4.23

Example 1

Claire read this problem.

Joe has 9 marbles. He has 3 times as many as Tim. How many does Tim have?

Claire multiplied 9 × 3 and got 27. Is this right? Explain your thinking.

Three Bean Salad Problems

There is a famous set of problems out of the Lawrence Hall of Science in Berkeley, California, that looks at developing algebraic reasoning through what is called three bean salad problems. Many people have taken this idea and done a great deal of work with it. I like the problems because they are engaging, hands-on, and rigorous. Students start out with simple problems that get progressively more difficult. See Figures 4.24 and 4.25 for examples.

Concept: Solving problems with manipulatives.
Workstation: Using the manipulatives to solve problems.

Figure 4.24

Example 1

There are 12 beans. There are 3 red beans. There are 4 more black-eyed peas than red beans. The rest are white beans. How many beans of each type are there?

1. Use the beans to solve.

2. Draw a sketch of the beans.

3. Make the sketch a bar diagram.

Figure 4.25

Example 2

There are 16 beans. Half of them are red beans. ¼ of them are white beans. The rest are black-eyed peas. How many beans of each are there?

1. Use the beans to solve.

2. Draw a sketch of the beans.

3. Make a bar diagram.

There are also coin puzzle problems that elicit the same type of reasoning but using coins as a pretext rather than beans (see Figure 4.26).

Figure 4.26

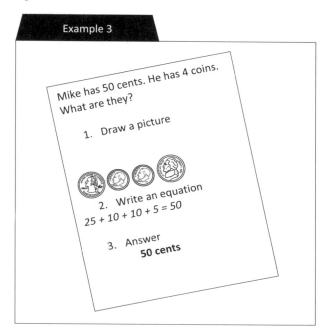

Example 3

Mike has 50 cents. He has 4 coins. What are they?

1. Draw a picture

2. Write an equation
   25 + 10 + 10 + 5 = 50

3. Answer
   50 cents

Word Problem Sort

In this workstation, the students sort the word problem by category (see Figures 4.27 and 4.28).

Concept: Identifying and sorting word problems.
Workstation: Read and sort word problems.

Figure 4.27

Example 1

Word Problem Sort	
Multiplication	Division
Sue had 5 bags with 5 marbles in each bag.	Maria had 16 cookies. She gave her sister half of the cookies.

Figure 4.28

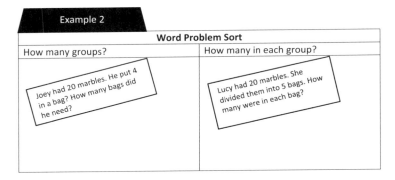

Example 2	
Word Problem Sort	
How many groups?	How many in each group?
Joey had 20 marbles. He put 4 in a bag? How many bags did he need?	Lucy had 20 marbles. She divided them into 5 bags. How many were in each bag?

Match and Concentration Match

There are different versions of concentration match. One version is where the students match the expression to the correct problem (see Figures 4.29 and 4.30).

Concept: Reasoning about word problems.
Workstation: Read and reason about word problems.

Figure 4.29

Example 1

Maribel had 3 bags and 5 rings in each bag. How many rings did she have altogether?

Circle the correct expression that represents this problem.

3 + 3 + 3   3 + 5

8 + 0   3 × 5

Figure 4.30

Example 2

David had 3 boxes. He had 15 cars. He put the same amount of cars in each box. How many cars did he put in each box?

Circle the correct expression that represents this problem.

3 + 15   15 ÷ 3

15 − 3   3 × 15

A different version is where the students match the word problem to the model (see Figure 4.31).

Figure 4.31

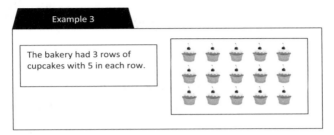

A third version is where the students match the word problem, the model, and the equation (see Figure 4.32).

Figure 4.32

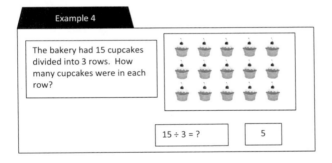

Teaching in the 21st Century

There is a plethora of tools that students can use to understand word problems (see Figure 4.33). Use the many different trade books to launch into problems. Provide opportunities for students to use both traditional and digital tools. Make sure students have toolkits.

Figure 4.33

Resources for Math Word Problem Workstation		
Picture Books/Stories	**Paper and Virtual Tools**	**Internet Word Problem Sites**
Use picture books as a launch into different problem contexts. There is a great book called *Tall Tale Math* by Betsy Franco specifically for grades 3–5 that mathematizes tall tales.	Use a variety of physical and virtual manipulatives to solve problems. For virtual manipulatives see: http://www.glencoe.com/ sites/common_assets/ mathematics/ebook_assets/ vmf/VMF-Interface.html	http://www.mathplaygroun d.com/thinkingblocks.html https://learnzillion.com/ http://gregtangmath.com/ wordproblems http://www.mathplaygroun d.com/wp_videos.html http://www.mathplaygroun d.com/ThinkingBlocks/think ing_blocks_start.html

Key Points

- CGI problems
- Beyond answer getting
- Rubrics and checklists
- Concrete, pictorial and abstract
- Various models
- Contextualizing
- Decontextualizing
- Two argument problems
- Find and fix the error
- Three bean salad problems
- Coin puzzle problems
- Word sorts
- Word problem concentration

Summary

Word problems are an essential part of the math curriculum. There are so many different ways to get students to get better at solving them. We need to offer a variety of opportunities for scaffolded practice. We should do them daily as a whole class routine and then provide workstations that students visit at least two or three times a week. Students should work alone, with partners, and in groups so that they can discuss their thinking, model their work, and follow the logic of others. It is crucial that students not only solve but also write word problems. It is essential that students gain the confidence to face word problems and move smoothly through them, knowing they are equipped with everything they need to successfully solve them.

Reflection Questions

1. Do you currently emphasize the process of problem solving, allowing time for students to unpack the problem, decide on a plan, follow the plan, check it a different way, and explain what they did?
2. How often do you give a word problem assessment to your students? Do you know what level problems your students should be working on?
3. How important are models in your current math curriculum?
4. What ideas stand out for you in this chapter?

References

Carpenter, T. P., Fennema, E., Franke, M. L., Levi, L., and Empson, S. B. (2014). *Children's mathematics: Cognitively guided instruction*, 2nd ed. Portsmouth, NH: Heinemann.

Franco, B. (2013). *Tall tale math: 12 Favorite tall tales with companion problems that build key math skills and concepts*. New York: Scholastic.

Ginsburg, H. P. (1987). The development of arithmetic thinking. In D. D. Hammill (Ed.), *Assessing the abilities and instructional needs of students* (pp. 423–440). Austin, TX: PRO-ED.

Lawrence Hall of Science. *Actividades de los Mateoyciencias*. Retrieved May 2015. http://lawrencehallofscience.org/sites/default/files/247science/mateoc/pdfs/activities_engl/Three_Bean_Salad.pdf.

Pólya, George (1957). *How to solve it*. Garden City, NY: Doubleday.

5

Vocabulary and Writing Workstations

Math is a language—if you don't know the words, then you can't speak it!

Big Ideas

Math is a language. It is important to be able to speak it, read it, write it, and to listen and understand it. Precision is very important.

Enduring Understandings

- Precise math words should be used to describe math.
- Students need to be able to communicate their thinking.
- Students should be able to understand the logic of others.

What it Means for a Workstation

The goal of the workstation is for students to have many opportunities to work with the vocabulary. They should be writing about math in their journals. They should be playing games with the vocabulary. If students don't know the words and the symbols to communicate in that language, then they will have a terrible time learning to speak it. We need to set up daily, weekly, and monthly routines to teach and assess vocabulary. Many of the routines should be done as a whole class activity first and then moved into math workstations.

Anchor Charts in the Workstation

There should definitely be math words up and around the room. Illustrated word walls that are preprinted but also done with the class and by individual groups are important (see Figures 5.1, 5.2, 5.3, 5.4, and 5.5).

Figure 5.1

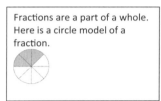

Fractions are a part of a whole. Here is a circle model of a fraction.

Figure 5.2

Did you use your math words?

Did you say **answer** *instead of* **quotient, product, sum, or difference?**

Did you say **number** *instead of* the math word? **Was it an addend, factor, dividend, divisor, subtrahend, or minuend?**

Figure 5.3

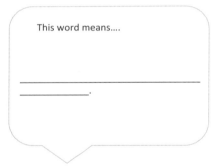

This word means....

_____
_____.

Figure 5.4

The opposite of this word is

Figure 5.5

An example of this word is _____.
A non-example of this word is _____.

Vocabulary Workstation Activities

Concentration Games

Concentration games are excellent games to put in the vocabulary math workstation. Students like these games, work well together in playing these games, and actually learn a great deal from them. These games allow for different levels, which is always a plus (see Figures 5.6 and 5.7).

Concept: Math vocabulary.
Workstation: Concentration match-up.

Figure 5.6

Concentration Version 1—Match the word and the Illustration
In this version of concentration, students match the word and the illustration.

| Mixed Number | 2½ |

Figure 5.7

Concentration Version 2—Match the word, the definition, and the illustration

| Mixed Number | 2½ | A whole number and a fraction. |

The Frayer Model

The Frayer model is an excellent graphic organizer to use in the math vocabulary workstation. Students can either complete one individually, with partners, or in groups. It requires students to think and explain their thinking, relate it to real life, and give examples and non-examples. This is also a good way to build a class-owned word wall—meaning that each partner pair is given a vocabulary word from the unit and they have to put it in a Frayer model and explain it to the class. Their work is what goes up on the word wall and now the class has built it and they actually understand the words and have much more ownership of it (see Figures 5.8 and 5.9).

Concept: Math vocabulary.
Workstation: Complete Frayer model.

Figure 5.8

Task Card I can discuss math vocabulary. Practice method: Frayer model Directions: Pick a word and complete the graphic organizer.	

Word Divisor Equation: $15 \div 3 = 5$	Definition The number that divides the dividend.
Real-Life Example Sue shared 10 marbles between her 4 friends. The divisor is 4 friends because the marbles are being shared among these 4 people.	Non-example Sue gave 4 friends 10 marbles each. How many marbles did she give away altogether? In this example we are multiplying instead of dividing.

Figure 5.9

Task Card
I can discuss math vocabulary.
Practice method: Frayer model
Directions: Pick a word, pick a box and *help your group complete* the graphic organizer. Each person uses a different color and on the back sign your name in that color.

Roles:
1   *Illustrator*
2   *Definition in your own words*
3   *Example giver*
4   *Non-example giver*
5   *Speaker/hang it up on word wall afterward*

Must have group consensus on all parts of the organizer.

Is-Can-Looks Like Charts

These are great charts to explain different concepts (see Figure 5.10). Students can do these either alone, with partners or in groups. It is always necessary in partners and groups to have an accountability measure so that nobody is hitchhiking. This could simply be having students work in a particular color and signing their name in that color on the project.

The following graphic organizer frame is good because it can be used with almost any topic.

Figure 5.10

Measurement			
Is	**Can**	**Requires**	**Looks Like**
How we show the size, length, or amount of things.	Help us to know how heavy something is, how much will fit in a container, or how long something is.	That we have the necessary tools to do the measuring. Scales, rulers, beakers.	Numbers about things. 500 ft 60 oz 5 km
Words about length and width and height: millimeters, centimeters, meters, inches, feet, yards **Distance: miles, kilometers** **Mass: gram, kilogram** **Weight: pounds, ounces** **Capacity: milliliters, liters, kiloliters**			

Guess My Word

Students play this game with partners. They pull a word from a bag and then have to give their partner clues to guess their word. The timer is set to two minutes. They have two minutes to get their partner to guess their word and get the team point. If they don't, the next team gets one chance to guess the word.

Tic-Tac-Toe

Tic-tac-toe games are familiar to students. They love to play tic-tac-toe. I do it in a variety of formats. I also play this game with the whole class before I introduce it into the workstations. In the whole-class format, the class is divided into two teams. They send someone up who picks a word. They are not the person who is on the hotspot, however; the team is responsible for answering questions about the word. If the team can answer all my questions, then the person can put an x or o. I play this from Kindergarten through 8th grade and all the students love it. In the workstation, students have a tic-tac-toe mat. They play with each other and they have to write the answers and illustrations on the side of the paper for accountability purposes (see Figures 5.11 and 5.12).

Concept: Math vocabulary.
Workstation: Vocabulary tic-tac-toe.

Figure 5.11

Task Card
I can describe and illustrate math vocabulary words.
Activity: Tic-tac-toe

Directions:
  1. Decide who goes first (rock-paper-scissors/dice roll/penny toss).
  2. Pick a word and describe it or illustrate it on the side of the paper.
  3. If your partner agrees, great! If they disagree and challenge you and they are correct, they get that word! If they are incorrect, the word is out of the game.
  4. Winner: Whoever gets three in a row first.

Figure 5.12

Polygon	Side	Angle
Triangle	Square	Trapezoid
Rectangle	Rhombus	Quadrangle

Small Group Charades

This game is similar to guess my word; however, in this game there is a caller. The caller pulls a word with key ideas and the teams have to try and guess their word. If they guess the word, that team gets the points. Whoever has the most points wins.

Vocabulary Bingo

In this version of bingo, all the cards are in a bag. The students take turns pulling the words, and if they are on their board, they get to mark them. The first person with four in a row or all four corners wins. This game is not as easy as it appears because the calling cards are made in a variety of ways. Some give the word, some give the definition, some give words that are the opposite, some give pictures (see Figure 5.13).

Concept: Math vocabulary.
Workstation: Bingo.

Figure 5.13

Divisor	Division Sign	Dividend	Factor
fraction	quotient	sum	addend
difference	multiple	product	column
minuend	subtrahend	row	subtraction

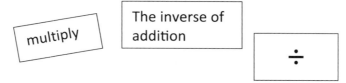

Word Finds

Students have to find and define vocabulary words. Students have to find the words (this is the hook). After they find a word, they have to define it and use it in a sentence (see Figure 5.14).

Concept: Math vocabulary.
Workstation: Word find and define.

Figure 5.14

Find the word. Write it here:	Define it in your own words.	Write a sentence using the word.
Find the word. Write it here:	Define it in your own words.	Write a sentence using the word.
Find the word. Write it here:	Define it in your own words.	Write a sentence using the word.

Crossword Puzzles

Crossword puzzles are great because students really have to think about the meaning of the word and use that understanding to do the puzzle. Students can work individually or with a partner. They can also do scaffolded (word bank) or un-scaffolded puzzles. To make crossword puzzles and word finds see: http://www.discoveryeducation.com/ free-puzzlemaker/?CFID=355277&CFTOKEN=12766806.

Other Writing Activities in the Workstation

Interactive Books

Students should do interactive notebooks throughout the year. They should keep these in a notebook so they can reference it whenever they need to. There should be some common models that are used often. Below are examples of three common, easy-to-make models that help to build conceptual understanding of a topic (see Figures 5.15, 5.16, 5.17, and 5.18).

Concept: Math vocabulary.
Workstation: Interactive notebooks.

Figure 5.15

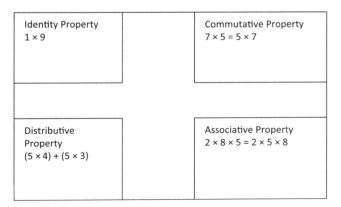

2 Flaps

Multiplication

Multiples	Factors

Figure 5.16

Post-it Book

Identity Property 1 × 9		Commutative Property 7 × 5 = 5 × 7
Distributive Property (5 × 4) + (5 × 3)		Associative Property 2 × 8 × 5 = 2 × 5 × 8

Figure 5.17

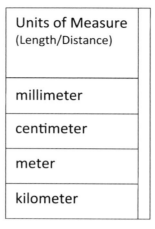

Units of Measure (Length/Distance)
millimeter
centimeter
meter
kilometer

Figure 5.18

Interactive journals are a great way to get students to create materials and tools that they can use throughout the year.

Look up math foldables on Pinterest.

http://www.rundesroom.com/2014/08/interactive-math-journal-faqs.html
https://www.pinterest.com/drnicki7/math-journals/

Look at Dinah Zikes Math foldables as well.

Two-Minute Essay

In this activity, students pick a task card and write everything they know about the chosen topic (which is usually about the unit of study—although sometimes there is review of other skills). They are encouraged to use numbers, words, and pictures. They usually write this in their math journal (see Figures 5.19 and 5.20). The students write for one minute. Then stop and review (30 seconds). Then they add something. Then they switch with a neighbor (for 30 seconds), who is expected to add something. Then, they get their essay back and have to add one more thing (30 seconds).

Concept: Math vocabulary.
Workstation: Two-minute essay.

Figure 5.19

Everything I know about fractions.

Figure 5.20

Everything I know about equivalent fractions.

Exemplar/Non-Exemplar Posters

Students illustrate *what it is* on one side and *what it is not* on the other side (see Figures 5.21 and 5.22). They should do this often because it is a very important part of conceptual understanding.

Concept: Math vocabulary.
Workstation: Exemplar/non-exemplar.

Figure 5.21

Name:	Date:
Polygon	**Not a Polygon**

Explanation: A polygon is a closed figure with straight sides, vertices, and angles. So, the triangle, trapezoid, and hexagon are all examples of polygons. The circle, the heart, and the half moon do not have sides, angles, and vertices; therefore, they are not polygons.

Figure 5.22

Name:	Date:
Even Number	**Not an Even Number**
4 xx xx	5 xx xx x
8 xx xx xx xx	3 xx x
10 xx xx xx xx xx	7 xx xx xx x

Explanation: An even number always can be paired. A number that is not even is missing a pair.

Strategy Book

Strategy books help students to explain different math fluency strategies (see Figure 5.23). These are great ways for students to process their thinking, give relevant examples, and show models of the strategies. It helps them to put names to the concepts they are using.

Concept: Math vocabulary.
Workstation: Strategy books.

Figure 5.23

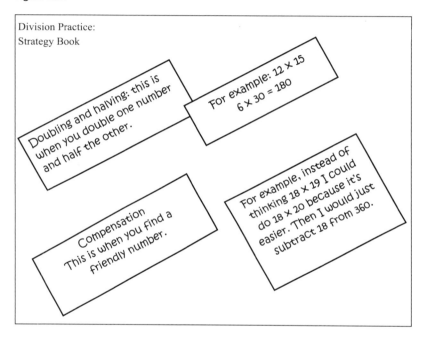

Graphic Organizers

Graphic organizers are such great tools for thinking to use in the writing and vocabulary workstation. Students should work as individuals, with partners, and in small groups to do these activities. Teachers should use the thinking maps throughout the various units. Different thinking maps help students to unpack concepts in different ways, but let's look at one that is always great to use (see Figures 5.24, 5.25, and 5.26).

Concept: Math vocabulary.
Workstation: Thinking maps.

Circle Maps

Figure 5.24

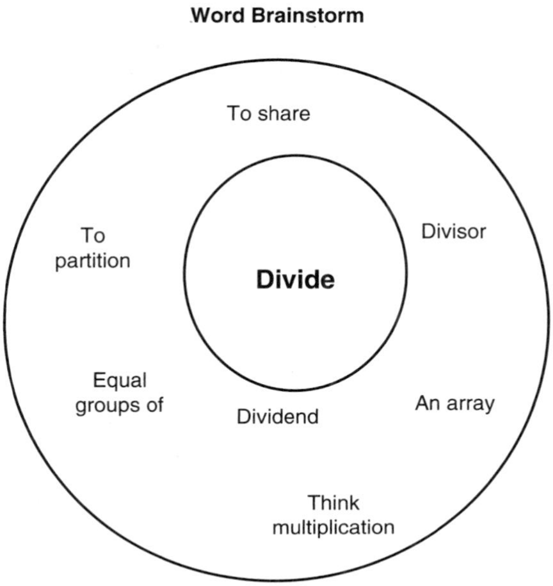

Word Brainstorm

To share

To partition

Divide

Divisor

Equal groups of

Dividend

An array

Think multiplication

Figure 5.25

Resources: Must cut and paste
http://mrwaddell.net/blog/uploadpics/Made4MathVocab--Reading-in-Math-research_116CA/Building.a.bridge.to.Academic.vocab.in.math.pdf

http://www.aea1.k12.ia.us/en/curriculum_instruction_and_assessment/math/english_language_learner_supports/math_vocabulary/

Concept: Math vocabulary.
Workstation: True or false sort.

Figure 5.26

True or False Sort

I can sort vocabulary cards
Task: Pick a card. Decide whether or not it is true or false. Sort the facts. Turn them over and verify if you are correct or not.

| The dividend is the amount that is being divided. | The quotient is the number being divided. |

True	False

Assessment

Don't forget to assess vocabulary. Assess at the beginning of the unit, throughout the unit with quick entrance and exit slips, and at the end of the unit. One way to do this is to have the students keep track of the words they are learning in a unit in a graphic organizer (see Figure 5.27).

Concept: Math vocabulary.
Workstation: Vocabulary chart.

Figure 5.27

Name: Kate Simon
Date: Dec. 21, 2015
Unit: Division

I can think about and use math vocabulary in context.

Word	Never Heard	Heard it or Seen it	I use this word (give an example)	
			Beginning of the Unit	End of the Unit
divide				
divisor				
dividend				
quotient				
share equally				
inverse operation				
multiplication				
groups of				
half				

Adapted from Partner in Education 2010 http://www.iceary.org/Conference/Differentiation. Conrad-Curry.pdf

Key Points
- Math vocabulary games: concentration, tic-tac-toe, and bingo
- Graphic organizers
- Interactive math journal booklets
- Two-minute essay
- Exemplar/non-exemplar posters
- Strategy books
- Word finds
- Crossword puzzles
- Thinking maps

Summary

Math vocabulary is one of the linchpins of a student's mathematical understanding. It is part of having a robust sense of numbers. Students need to be able to describe and illustrate the concepts they are learning and, therefore, they need the words. Vocabulary practice should be an ongoing structure in the classroom, with students working individually, with partners, and in groups. Students should be excited about the ways in which they are learning the vocabulary and interested in knowing more. Most of all, students must use these words in their daily discussions and so must the teacher!

Reflection Questions

1. How often do you play vocabulary games as a whole class?
2. What might you try right away to get your students practicing math vocabulary?
3. In what ways might you integrate some of the writing activities into your units of study?
4. What sticks out the most for you in this chapter?

6

Digital Workstations

> If we teach today as we taught yesterday, we rob our children of tomorrow.
>
> (Dewey, 1916)

Big Ideas

We live in the 21st century! The International Society for Technology in Education (2007) has defined the following standards for 21st-century students:

- Creativity and innovation
- Communication and collaboration
- Research and information
- Critical thinking, problem solving, and decision making
- Digital citizenship
- Technology operations

Enduring Understandings

- Students will understand that there are many ways to use technology in math class, including using digital math tools to think through, explain, and show mathematical concepts.
- Students will be creative and not only consume but also produce knowledge on the internet.
- Students will understand that they can share information, teach each other concepts, and collaborate with others online.
- Students will understand that they can "plan and conduct research, manage projects [and] solve problems. . . . Using digital

tools and resources" (International Society for Technology in Education, 2007).

- Students will "demonstrate personal responsibility for lifelong learning" (International Society for Technology in Education, 2007).

What it Means for a Workstation

The students that we teach are called Generation Z and the Alpha Generation (Williams, 2015a and 2015b). These are the generations born in a world where the internet always existed. The digital workstation is meant to remind us that we live in the 21st century. It is not exactly a place, although it can be. It is more of an idea about a way of doing math and communicating with each other. The idea of a *must-have digital workstation* is that we live in a digital world and work with "digital natives," as Prensky (2001) calls them. We are called the "immigrants." We must tailor our classroom to the ways that students learn. I am not saying that everything should be digital, because I don't think it should. But I am saying that some things should be. There should be at least one, and ideally more than one, space where students can work with digital technologies of the 21st century—virtual tools, games, videos. So tech up!

Setting Up Folders

There are many different activities for students to do on laptops. Some of them are bought programs while others are free and accessible on the internet. The question becomes how do we organize these things in ways that are easy to reach and keep students from getting off track doing things that they shouldn't be doing? One way to address this is to have the sites organized in a LiveBinder or a portaportal. These are spaces to organize information so that students can go right there and push a button and end up where they belong. Both of these systems can be private or public. Teachers can send the passwords home so that parents/guardians and students can access the sites from home.

- LiveBinders are like electronic binders. They are organized by files. The files can be named and organized so students just go into them and click on the website where they are supposed to be working. See here for an example: http://www.livebinders.com/.
- Portaportals are like electronic file cabinets. They are easy to make and organize. Teachers can differentiate the material in different files. See here for an example: http://www.portaportal.com/.

Tools

There are many virtual tools online so that students can explore concepts from the operations to fractions. The National Library of Virtual Manipulatives is a great library that helps to build conceptual understanding and procedural fluency (see new app at https://www.mattimath.com/). Glencoe is another really fantastic site that is organized by grade levels, tools, story mats, and other things (http://www.glencoe.com/sites/com mon_assets/mathematics/ebook_assets/vmf/VMF-Interface.html).

Math Learning Center has recently put out several FREE apps that work across platforms! Yeaaaaa! Check them out here: http://catalog. mathlearningcenter.org/apps.

12 Types of Activities to Do at the Digital Workstation

1. Fluency Games

Fluency games are really important. They can be played in the fluency workstation as well as in the digital workstation. Meaning, in the digital workstation there can be a menu of fluency games that students work on. But also, in the fluency workstation there can be digital games integrated into the menu of activities. It can work either one or both ways. However it is done, students should have an opportunity to practice the designated fluencies using the web. Here are a few of my favorite sites:

- Math Playground http://www.mathplayground.com/
- Johnnnie's Homepage http://jmathpage.com/
- BBC http://www.bbc.co.uk/bitesize/ks2/maths/
- Math Play http://www.math-play.com/
- Fluency Games http://www.multiplication.com/games/all-games

2. Specific Unit of Study Games

Besides the four must-have stations, there are the specific unit of study stations, such as fractions, decimals, measurement, and data. There are plenty of games for students to practice different concepts. Here are a few places to do that:

- http://www.mathplayground.com/
- http://jmathpage.com/
- http://www.math-play.com/

3. Vocabulary Games

Here are two ideas for working on math vocabulary in the digital workstation. First, Spelling City is a great place for students to practice vocabulary. It's free but you have to register. Students can take a spelling test, a vocabulary test, play games, do flashcards, and do a *teach me* segment. If you upgrade there are even more games. Check it out at: http://www.spellingcity.com/math-vocabulary.html.

The second place is to go to puzzlemaker.com and have students create their own math vocabulary word finds and crossword puzzles as an activity or assessment. They must also create the answer keys. They can then put these in the vocabulary workstation for other students to work on. Students love to do this. It takes a bit of scaffolding (like providing the list of words to choose from) but they can do it, they like to do it, and they learn a great deal from doing it.

4. Word Problems

As with fluency, so with word problems, the students can either do some web-based activities in the word problem workstation or in the digital workstation. There are some great sites for students to practice word problems. Math playground has *Thinking Blocks*, where they can work through a series of models for tape diagramming problems based on the operation. This is a fantastic site. (Math Playground: http://www.mathplayground. com/ThinkingBlocks/thinking_blocks_start.html.)

Greg Tang has also recently built a whole world of word problem activities where students can pick the word problem by type and even get hints about how to set up the problem with tape diagrams. If the students do one problem at a time, they can get the hints and the answers. This is how I recommend that they practice. There is also an option to generate several word problems at a time, but these just give the word problems without all of the scaffolding. (Greg Tang Word Problem Generator: http://gregtang math.com/wordproblems.)

5. iPads and iPods

There are so many great math apps out there. Here are a few favorites:

- Splash Math Bingo
- Mathmateer
- Sushi Monster
- Penguin Math
- Math Circus

6. PowerPoint, Prezi, and Voicethread

(These are both programs that you have to pay for but they do have school pricing.)
It is very important that we start students using presentation methods early on because this is all part of being a public mathematician and presenting, defending, and being proud of one's work. Having the tools to do this is important. Our students will grow up to work with teams around the world on global platforms. The present-day technologies will be obsolete by then, most likely, but the big ideas of presenting information in an organized manner, making work interesting, engaging, presenting error free work, and being able to discuss it knowledgeably are skills that will last them a lifetime.

PowerPoint, Prezi (takes PowerPoint to the next level with swirling text and close-up and back-away imaging), and Voicethread (public PowerPoints where folks can see it and comment on it with avatars) are some great ways to get started. Check them out at these websites: Prezi—https:// prezi.com/prezi-for-education/; Voicethread—https://voicethread.com.

7. Videos—Flipping It

Students making videos of their understanding of math concepts is great. They learn as they teach. They get very serious very quickly about what they are putting out there. They know an authentic audience when they see one. In this activity, students would design a teaching video. Of course, the teacher with the students should make a criteria list and a rubric so it's not a free-for-all. But there is good teaching and good learning to be had from flipped videos. You can do this on iPads and video cameras. You can buy Flip cameras, which are pretty affordable now as well. Once you have the videos, put them up on your blog or your school website so other members of your community can see them and learn from them. Imagine a parent clicking on a student-made video to learn what "doubling and halving" looks like.

8. Podcasts

Students should be encouraged to create their own podcasts as well. I have seen students do some incredible podcasting, even in 1st grade. Students develop a script about what they want to discuss and then do it. Here is a great article about how to do it with students: http://www.readingrockets. org/article/creating-podcasts-your-students.

9. Glogs

Glogs are really fun. Glogs are like science board posters on steroids. They are basically a digital version of a poster project. They are way cooler because you can link videos, songs, and Flip videos, and insert games and assessments. Teachers can make them for students to explore a concept at the digital workstation or in individual designated stations (such as fluency or fractions). Also, the upper elementary students should be given the opportunity to make some. They are easy to make and yet are quite cognitively demanding. Given the correct criteria the task can be designed at a DOK Level 4. Students usually do them with a partner or group. Of course, there should be criteria and rubrics (http://edu.glogster.com/). Be sure to look at the Glogopedia math section for examples.

10. Animotos

Animotos are great, quick, easy-to-make commercial-like videos that can be used to discuss a particular topic. Students can make them and then discuss what images they chose and why. They are a great part of an overall presentation about a topic. Basically, students put together a visual collage of images about a topic (say fractions or measurement) and then the Animoto mixes them together and plays them back in a 30-second video. Every time the video changes the images around. Students can add music, and it is this great visual experience that shows knowledge of a topic. Of course, the Animoto must be followed up with a presentation or paper that explains the chosen images. See more here (they have school pricing): https://guided-math.wordpress.com/2010/08/27/animoto-and-guided-math-lessons/.

11. 3D Pens

These are new and cool and relatively inexpensive. 3D pens allow the person to create 3D images with a wax and a type of heat gun. Students can either make or download outlines of things and then trace them in and they dry and then students build them. So, for instance, they could make or print out geometric nets and then color them in with a 3D pen and then construct the 3D figure. They are amazing! Check them out here: http://the3doodler.com/.

12. 3D Printers

3D printers are the future. They are just now beginning to be explored in schools but they are where we are going. You can create so many things with 3D printers. They allow students to be creative, innovative, and precise. Students create designs, applying the math they need for the project, and then put them in the 3D printer and voila—out pops the thing—a phone case, a pencil holder, a bird feeder. It's supercalifragilisticexpialidocious! Only a few schools have them yet, but get one. Write a grant like the teacher in this video did: https://www.youtube.com/watch?v=eLVFsj7szo4.

Key Points

- Digital natives
- LiveBinders and portaportals
- Digital fluency games
- Digital unit of study games
- Digital vocabulary games
- Digital word problems
- iPads and iPods—math apps
- PowerPoint, Prezi, and Voicethread
- Flip videos
- Podcasts
- Glogs
- Animotos
- 3D pens
- 3D printers

Summary

Technology is part of the landscape of our daily lives. We have to embrace it and integrate it in meaningful ways into our classrooms so that our digital natives can thrive. Organization is key, so get a system. Games are essential, so pick a few that you like. Pick some fluency games, some vocabulary games, and some good apps (not all games or apps are created equal . . . be choosy). Let students build word problem power online. Let them learn to be confident, competent, public thinkers using different technologies such as PowerPoints, Prezis, Voicethreads, videos, podcasts, Glogs, and Animotos. Most of all, teach them that math is useful. Let them use it by creating things with 3D pens and 3D printers. Live it, love it, learn it!

Reflection Questions

1. In what ways do your workstations reflect that you teach digital natives that live in the 21st century?
2. What are some new ideas for you in this chapter? What are you thinking right now?
3. What is one digital upgrade that you might give your classroom?

References

Dewey, J. (1916). *Democracy and education.* New York: Free Press
International Society for Technology in Education. (2007). *National educational technology standards for students.* Retrieved from http://www.iste.org/standards/iste-standards/standards-for-students.
Prensky, M. (2001). "Digital natives, digital immigrants." *On the Horizon* 9, no. 5, 1–6.
Williams, A. (2015a). "Meet alpha: The next (next) generation." *New York Times.* http://www.nytimes.com/2015/09/19/fashion/meet-alpha-the-next-next-generation.html?_r=0.
Williams, A. (2015b). Move over Millennials, here comes Generation Z. *New York Times.* http://www.nytimes.com/2015/09/20/fashion/move-over-millennials-here-comes-generation-z.html.

Part III

Additional Unit-Specific Workstations (or Units of Study)

7

Place Value Workstations

Place value is the basis for a robust sense of number!

Big Ideas

We use a base ten system.

Enduring Understandings

- Numbers can be represented using objects, words, and symbols.
- There are many ways to represent a number with ones, tens, hundreds, etc.
- There are different models and tools to represent numbers.

What it Means for a Workstation

The goal of the workstation is for students to have many opportunities to work with place value. I have recently been telling people that I think this should actually be a permanent workstation, given the nature of the place value gaps that many students are experiencing these days. Done this way, there would be a series of leveled activities from the prior grades up until the current grade. In this way the teacher could have the students reviewing the trouble spots on an ongoing basis.

Either way, students should be building models, sketching models, and putting together and pulling apart numbers in a variety of ways. They should be playing games that make them use a variety of strategies for working with multi-digit numbers. We need to set up daily, weekly, and monthly routines to teach and assess place value. Many of the routines should be done as a whole-class activity first and then moved into math workstations.

This chapter shows several different types of activities to put at the place value workstation. By no means does it cover all the place value topics in 3rd through 5th grade. For one thing, the operation aspect of place value was discussed in detail as part of the fluency workstation. Moreover, decimals are so important that they were given their own chapter. What this chapter does do though is show a variety of formats to engage students around the big ideas and enduring understandings of place value.

Anchor Charts in the Workstation

There should definitely be place value anchor charts around the room. There should be place value charts with examples (see Figure 7.1).

Figure 7.1

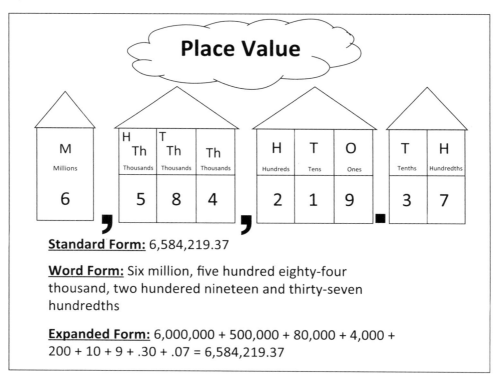

Example Place Value Workstations

Understanding Place and Value

Students should do a great deal of work looking at the word form, expanded form, and models for making numbers. There are many different activities and games that students can do to build their understanding. The activities where students have to generate a number and then show it in many forms are good for ongoing practice. Here are a few (see Figures 7.2, 7.3, 7.4, 7.5, 7.6, and 7.7).

Concept: There are many different ways to represent a number.
Workstation: Roll and show/pull and show.

Either use place value dice or assign different color dice different places. Students can also pull cards and make numbers.

Figure 7.2

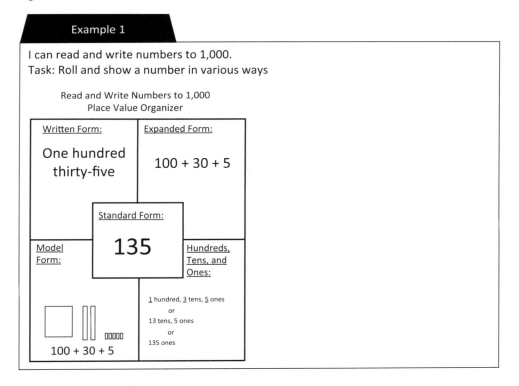

Example 1

I can read and write numbers to 1,000.
Task: Roll and show a number in various ways

Read and Write Numbers to 1,000
Place Value Organizer

Written Form:	Expanded Form:
One hundred thirty-five	100 + 30 + 5

Standard Form:

135

Model Form:

Hundreds, Tens, and Ones:

1 hundred, 3 tens, 5 ones
or
13 tens, 5 ones
or
135 ones

100 + 30 + 5

Place Value Match Games

Place value match games are fun! Students like them. There are different levels. One level is to have the students match the number and the expanded form, another level is to have the students match the above and the word form (see Figure 7.3).

Figure 7.3

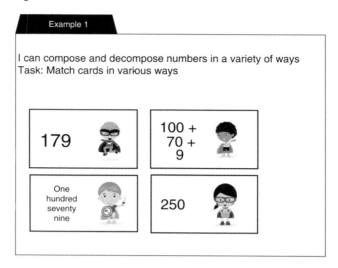

Place Value Mats

Place value mats with pictures are important because they provide a graphic organizer for students to see the numbers in a different way. They help students to organize their thinking about the numbers.

Concept: Numbers in the base ten system have a place and a value.
Workstation: Practice expanded form with an illustrated chart.

Figure 7.4

Example 1

I can show numbers in a variety of ways.
Task: Build numbers and record them

Place	Thousands	Hundreds	Tens	Ones
Model (Build it)				◊
Sketch it				
Write it in expanded form				
Write the word name				

For work specifically on expanded form, students can work with the place value cups or flags. Students should have some sort of manipulative for place value. Place value cups are easy and great. You take the number of cups you need based on the grade level. Write on each set of cups in a specific color. The students should make the cups themselves.

Building Conceptual Understanding of Place Value

Place Value Cups

Concept: Numbers in the base ten system have a place and a value.
Workstation: Practice expanded form with cups.

Figure 7.5

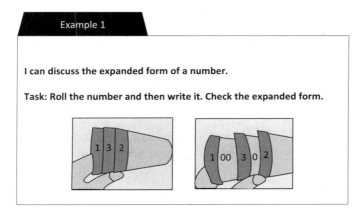

Place Value Cards

The place value cards are great. More and more people are starting to use them. They are excellent because they allow the students to see the actual value of the numbers.

Concept: Numbers in the base ten system have a place and a value.
Workstation: Practice expanded form with number cards.

Figure 7.6

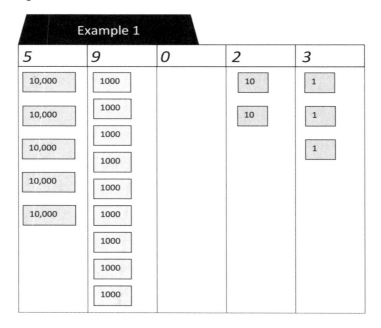

Here is a different version of the place value cards.

Concept: Numbers in the base ten system have a place and a value.
Workstation: Practice expanded form with number cards.

Figure 7.7

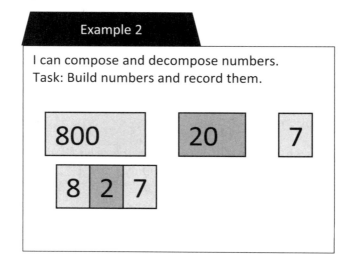

Here is a chart that students would fill in with any number that they chose. They would then have to fill in the amounts and write it in expanded form.

Concept: Numbers in the base ten system have a place and a value.
Workstation: Practice expanded form with chart and number cards.

Figure 7.8

Example 3			
I can compose and decompose numbers. Task: Build numbers and record them.			
5 thousands	**7** hundreds	**2** tens	**1** ones
1000	100	10	1
1000	100	10	1
1000	100		1
1000	100		1
1000	100		
	100		
	100		
5000 +	700 +	20 +	4
5 x 1000	7 x 100	2 x 10	4 x 1

Place Value Books

It is always good to have students write their own books explaining the topic. They can do this in a variety of ways. Here is one example. Students should be given the criteria and then they have to write everything in their own words (see Figures 7.9 and 7.10).

Figure 7.9

Example 1

Chart

Millions	Hundred Thousands	Ten Thousands	Thousands	Hundreds	Tens	Ones
1	9	5	8	2	8	9

Figure 7.10

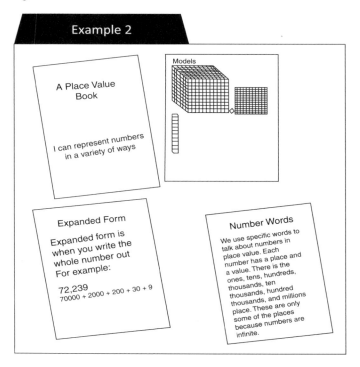

More Games

There are many topics in place value. Students tend to have a variety of gaps. In the place value workstation, I recommend that teachers use a variety of concept and skill games from prior grade levels because students are often shaky or entirely missing some of the ideas (see Figures 7.11, 7.12, 7.13, 7.14, 7.15, and 7.16).

Figure 7.11

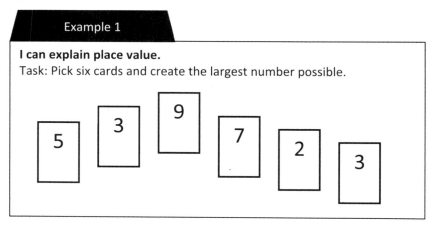

Comparing Numbers

Figure 7.12

Example 1

I can compare numbers.
Task: Each person rolls five dice. Make the largest number possible. Then, compare the two numbers using the symbols >, <, =.

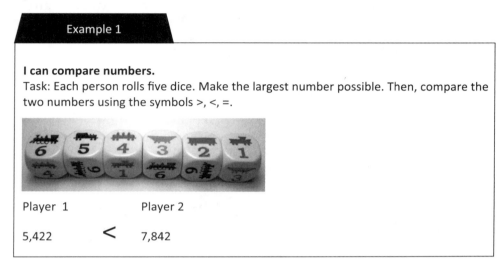

Player 1   Player 2

5,422   **<**   7,842

Rounding Numbers

Students should use number line visuals, number lines, and number grids to round numbers. Make sure that students have different sizes of these tools.

Figure 7.13

Example 1

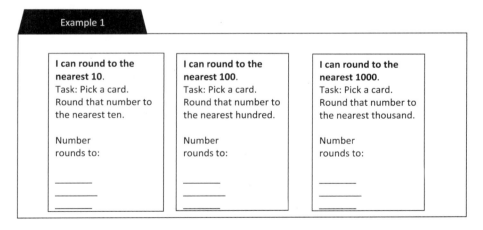

I can round to the nearest 10.	I can round to the nearest 100.	I can round to the nearest 1000.
Task: Pick a card. Round that number to the nearest ten.	Task: Pick a card. Round that number to the nearest hundred.	Task: Pick a card. Round that number to the nearest thousand.
Number rounds to:	Number rounds to:	Number rounds to:
_____	_____	_____
_____	_____	_____
_____	_____	_____

Gameboards

There are a variety of different types of gameboards that students can practice concepts on. Some games they can play with a partner or group and other games they can play by themselves. There should always be an answer key so students can check their work (see Figures 7.14 and 7.15.)

Figure 7.14

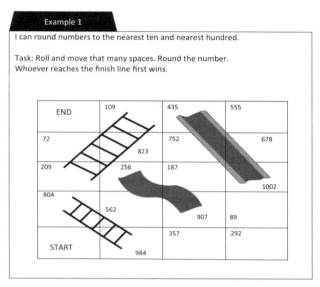

Figure 7.15

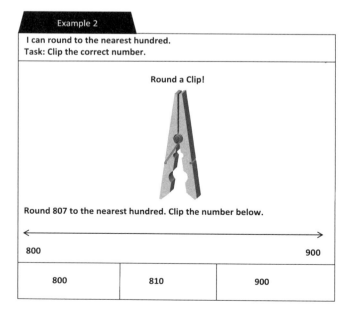

Culminating Activities

At the end of the unit there are different learning structures to help students review and show their understanding of the concepts. Here are these structures with place value examples.

Choice Boards

It is important to give students choice boards so that they can choose ways to demonstrate their learning of the content. In this particular board, the students have to choose two things, make a plan with some deadlines, and follow the rubrics to complete the plan.

Figure 7.16

Choice Board		
You must choose two things from the board to do by the end of the unit. You can work on these projects in your workstations and at home. Please submit your plan to Ms. Thomas by next Wednesday, February 18th. Be sure to look at the specific rubric for your projects.		
Make a poster about place value.	Make a Glog about place value.	Design your own project about place value.
Make a board game to practice place value.	Write an essay about place value. Use numbers, words, and pictures.	Make a PowerPoint about place value.
Do the *Find Someone Who Can* board.	Make a card game to practice rounding numbers.	Make a podcast about place value.

Figure 7.17

My Plan for Place Value Projects

Week 1:
First, I will work on the poster project. I am going to do this by myself. I will do this in the Vocabulary/Writing workstation.

Week 2:
Then I will work on the card game for rounding. I will also do this in the Vocabulary/Writing workstation. I am going to design the game in a group.

Find Someone Who is more like a group review where several people are involved and everybody is learning.

True or false sorts allow the students to reason about the learned concepts. These tend to be tricky for students and require that they stop, concentrate, and then make thinking decisions before they choose an answer.

Figure 7.18

Place Value: Find Someone Who Can...		
I understand place value. I can discuss different place value topics. Task: During project choice time take the board and find different people to fill in your board. Each person must sign their name and prove that they can do the task. They can either write it on the board or on another piece of paper. Each person can only answer one time.		
Write down 4 numbers that can round to 1000. Signature:	Write a 6-digit number in standard form and expanded notation. Signature:	Write down 3 numbers that round down to 1000. Signature:
Multiply two 2-digit numbers in 2 different ways. Signature:	Divide 456/7 in 2 different ways. Signature:	Write down 3 numbers that can round to 100,000. Signature:
Solve: 4567 + 399 in two different ways. Signature:	Solve: 5000 -789 Signature:	Write 3 different statements to compare 2 different 5 digit numbers using the symbols >, <, =. Signature:

Figure 7.19

True or False Sort	
I can sort place value statements. Task: Pick a card. Decide whether or not it is true or false. Sort the facts. Turn them over and verify if you are correct or not.	

$67 = (6 \times 10) + (7 \times 1)$	$4{,}242 > (4 \times 1000) + (2 \times 10) + (4 \times 100) + (2 \times 1)$

True	False

Teaching in the 21st Century

There is a plethora of resources that students can use to understand place value (see Figure 7.20). Be sure to read the books about big numbers and small numbers. Teach them some of the songs. Be sure to download the base ten block paper and the ten thousand grid paper so they can represent numbers with these tools. Have the students play some of the internet games.

Figure 7.20

Place Value Resources			
Picture Books	**Videos/Songs**	**Paper and Virtual Tools**	**Internet Games**
Sir Circumference and All the King's Tens by Cindy Neuschwander	Look up place value by grade on Learnzillion.com	http://www.topmarks.co.uk/Interactive.aspx?cat=21	http://www.math-play.com/place-value-games.html
Earth Day Hooray by Stuart J. Murphy		http://www.glencoe.com/sites/common_assets/mathematics/ebook_assets/vmf/VMF-Interface.html	http://www.starrmatica.com/standalone/starrMaticaplaceValueMysteryNumbers.swf
How Big is a Million? by Anna Milbourne and Serena Riglietti	https://www.youtube.com/watch?v=gsvrhKka1nc	https://www-k6.thinkcentral.com/content/hsp/math/hspmath/na/gr3-5/itools_intermediate_9780547274058_/basetenblocks.html	
How Much is A Million? by David M. Schwartz and Steven Kellogg	https://www.youtube.com/watch?v=bWgZsJmATsl		http://www.funbrain.com/tens/
A Million Dots by Andrew Clements and Mike Reed		http://nlvm.usu.edu/en/nav/grade_g_2.html	
Big Numbers by Edward Packard		https://www.teacherspayteachers.com/Product/Printable-Place-Value-Tools-751096	http://www.quia.com/mc/279741.html
Little Numbers by Edward Packard		Use the base ten paper and the ten thousand grid. Must cut and paste url: http://www.ablongman.com/vandewalleseries/Vol_3_BLM_PDFs/V3%20All%20BLMs.pdf	http://www.learnalberta.ca/content/me3us/flash/lessonLauncher.html?lesson=lessons/03/m3_03_00_x.swf
A Place for Zero by Phyllis Hornung			
One Grain of Rice: A Mathematical Folktale by Demi			http://www.topmarks.co.uk/Interactive.aspx?cat=21
Zero by Kathryn Otoshi			
How Much, How Many, How Far, How Heavy, How Long, How Tall Is 1000? by Helen Nolan			http://www.math-play.com/Place-Value-Millionaire/place-value-millionaire.html
Can you Count to a Googol by Robert E. Wells			http://www.math-play.com/place-value-games.html
*Also see **https://www.pinterest.com/drnicki7/place-value/**			

Key Points

- Represent numbers (objects, words, and symbols)
- Place and value of numbers
- Standard form, word form, and expanded form
- Different models and tools
- Order numbers
- Symbols to compare numbers
- Round numbers

Summary

Place value is about understanding the pattern of our number system. Students understand pattern when they can see it and feel it. It is very important to get students to build and discuss the pattern. Students should build it and sketch it. Using a variety of hands-on tools in engaging ways coupled with sketches furthers understanding and are ways to launch the unit. If this is done, then students can use the expanded form with understanding. Use the visual tools so that students can expand out the number with place value notation. Games are important for students to practice and use their understanding in engaging and purposeful ways.

Reflection Questions

1. How often do you spend time on getting students to visualize and build place value concepts (yes, even in 3rd, 4th, and 5th grade)?
2. Do you use the visual expanded form cards with your students? If so, how? If not, how might you start?
3. Do you currently give your students different opportunities to show their understanding besides formalized end of chapter tests?

8

Fraction Workstations

One of our main math missions is to get our kids on friendly terms with fractions!

Big Ideas

Fractions are numbers that we use in our everyday lives to represent numbers less than a whole.

Enduring Understandings

- Fractions describe the division of a whole (regions, set, segment) into equal parts.
- The numerator (tells how many equal parts are indicated) and the denominator tell how many equal parts.
- The whole must be specified.
- Fractions can be named in different ways.
- Fractions can be used to compare a part to the whole.
- Fractions can be added and subtracted just like whole numbers.
- There are many different models for operating on fractions.

What it Means for a Workstation

The goal of the fraction workstation is for students to work with and get on friendly terms with fractions. Students should play board games, card games, dice games, and domino games throughout the year (constantly reviewing the material from the year before) as well as adding current grade level concepts. The fraction workstation activities should require a great deal of work with concrete manipulatives as well as many pictorial

◆ 117

activities. This chapter is meant to give you plenty of examples of the types of activities that students should be engaging in at the fraction workstation. It does not cover every topic about fractions from grades 3–5. It does give the general structures for the activities and games that should take place across fraction topics in the workstation.

Anchor Charts in the Workstation

There should be plenty of anchor charts up that illustrate the different topics. The students should make their own versions of many of these and put them in their math journals for future reference (see Figures 8.1 and 8.2). There should definitely be math words up and around the room. Word walls should be illustrated and oftentimes done by the students.

Figure 8.1

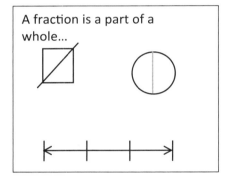

Figure 8.2

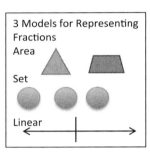

Tools to Teach

There should be a variety of tools used for teaching fractions. Fractions should be modeled with the area model, the set model, and the linear model. Fraction bars should be a main tool in the toolkit because it is a great linear model (see Figure 8.3). Students should make their own set of

Figure 8.3

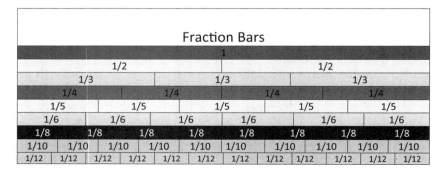

fraction bars by folding and cutting paper. After they have done that, they can also be given fraction bar templates that are labeled and unlabeled as well as the actual plastic fraction bars and towers. The bars are horizontal and the towers are vertical.

Number Lines

There are many different types of fraction number lines that should be explored throughout a unit of study and hung up all year long (see Figure 8.4). There should be a blank number line that students can use to plot fractions on. There should be a number line with half marked on it. There should be number lines that parallel the fraction bars. There should be number lines that show where improper fractions are located. There should be number lines with mixed numbers. The goal is that students see these number lines, are familiar with these number lines, and can use them to

Figure 8.4

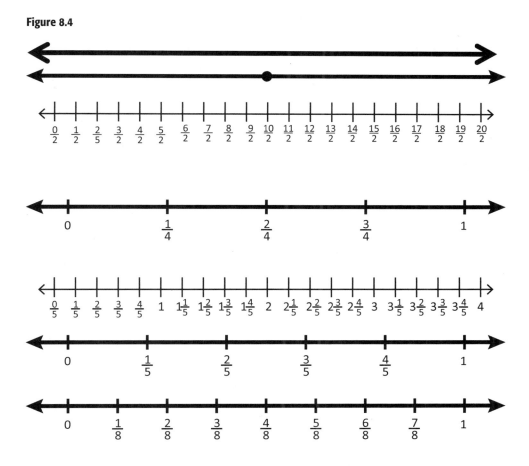

think and reason about fractions. A set should be hung up in the classroom and then the students should have their own set in their fraction toolkit.

Fraction squares, circles, and pattern blocks are other great tools. Be sure to use the paper templates (both labeled and unlabeled) as well as the concrete manipulatives (see Figures 8.5, 8.6, 8.7, 8.8, 8.9, and 8.10).

Fraction Squares

The individual rectangle in each box is the whole.

Figure 8.5

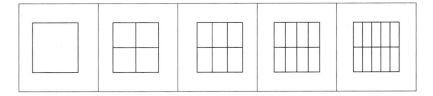

Fraction Circles

Figure 8.6

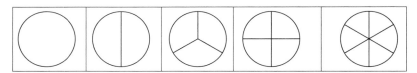

A Little Peace of Africa by Laine Sutherland

Pattern Blocks

Figure 8.7

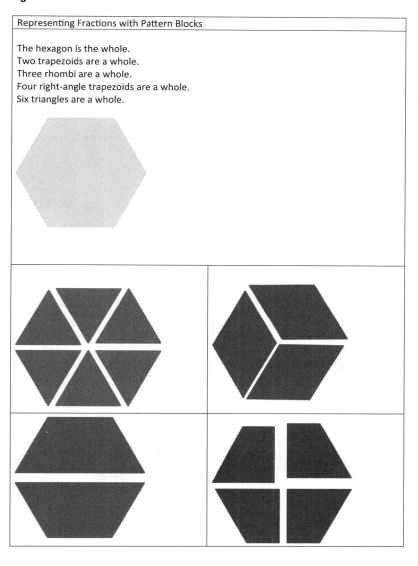

Representing Fractions with Pattern Blocks

The hexagon is the whole.
Two trapezoids are a whole.
Three rhombi are a whole.
Four right-angle trapezoids are a whole.
Six triangles are a whole.

Fraction Workstations

Showing Fractions

Concept: Building an understanding of a fraction as part of a whole.
Workstation: Draw fractions.

Figure 8.8

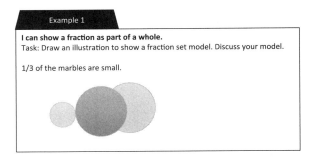

> **Example 1**
>
> **I can show a fraction as part of a whole.**
> Task: Draw an illustration to show a fraction set model. Discuss your model.
>
> 1/3 of the marbles are small.

Equivalent Fractions

Concept: Building an understanding of equivalent fractions.
Workstations: Generate equivalent fractions (Figures 8.8, 8.9, 8.10, and 8.11).

Figure 8.9

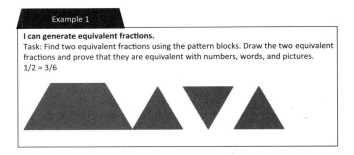

> **Example 1**
>
> **I can generate equivalent fractions.**
> Task: Find two equivalent fractions using the pattern blocks. Draw the two equivalent fractions and prove that they are equivalent with numbers, words, and pictures.
> 1/2 = 3/6

Figure 8.10

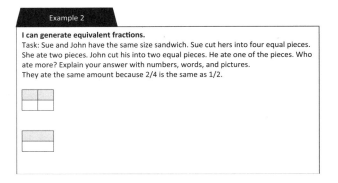

> **Example 2**
>
> **I can generate equivalent fractions.**
> Task: Sue and John have the same size sandwich. Sue cut hers into four equal pieces. She ate two pieces. John cut his into two equal pieces. He ate one of the pieces. Who ate more? Explain your answer with numbers, words, and pictures.
> They ate the same amount because 2/4 is the same as 1/2.

Equivalent Fractions on the Multiplication Table

Here is a way to look at equivalent fractions with the multiplication table. When I use it with students, I start with a half table so that students can focus. Use this table after doing a lot of work at the concrete and pictorial level. This is the abstract level.

Concept: Building an understanding of comparing and ordering fractions.
Workstations: Equivalent fractions.

Figure 8.11

Example 1											
The Multiplication Table											
Look at this table and discuss the patterns.											
Look across any two connected numbers and see the equivalent fraction table.											
1	2	3	4	5	6	7	8	9	10	11	12
2	4	6	8	10	12	14	16	18	20	22	24
3	6	9	12	15	18	21	24	27	30	33	36
4	8	12	16	20	24	28	32	36	40	44	48
5	10	15	20	25	30	35	40	45	50	55	60
6	12	18	24	30	36	42	48	54	60	66	72

Comparing and Ordering Fractions

Too often students are rushed to order and compare fractions as an abstract activity. There should be plenty of opportunities for students to use Play-Doh, paper cutting, and drawing to make and compare fractions. After several of these experiences, students should *then* move into comparing numbers abstractly. Here are some examples of tasks that students can do in this workstation (see Figures 8.12, 8.13, 8.14, and 8.15).

Figure 8.12

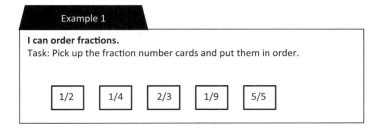

Example 1

I can order fractions.
Task: Pick up the fraction number cards and put them in order.

1/2   1/4   2/3   1/9   5/5

Figure 8.13

Example 2

I can order fractions.
Task: Roll the dice 5 times. The green dice is the numerator and the yellow dice is the denominator. Draw a number line and put the fractions in order on the number line.

⟵──────────────────────⟶

Figure 8.14

Example 3

I can compare fractions on a number line.
Task 1: Pull five fraction cards. Draw a number line and put the fractions in order on the number line.

6/7   4/8   3/4

3/3   1/2

Task 2: Compare the fractions using the symbols =, <, >.

Figure 8.15

Example 4

I can order fractions
Task: Use the visual models below. First label the fraction for each model. Draw a number line and order the fractions.*

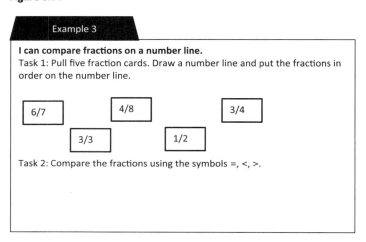

* This is an advanced task. A less advanced task would be to have the figures already labeled.

Anchor charts help students to understand how to compare numbers. Students should have to make their own notes and keep them in their folders. The workstation would give the students different fractions to compare (generated from fractions cards, dice, and dominos) and then have them explain how they chose to compare them using the anchor chart as a scaffold (see Figure 8.16).

Figure 8.16

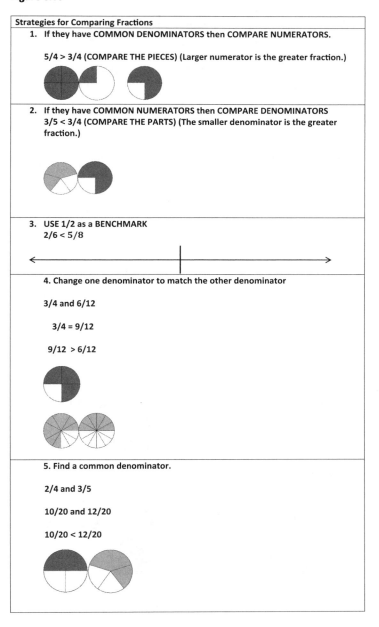

Strategies for Comparing Fractions

1. If they have COMMON DENOMINATORS then COMPARE NUMERATORS.

    5/4 > 3/4 (COMPARE THE PIECES) (Larger numerator is the greater fraction.)

2. If they have COMMON NUMERATORS then COMPARE DENOMINATORS
   3/5 < 3/4 (COMPARE THE PARTS) (The smaller denominator is the greater fraction.)

3. USE 1/2 as a BENCHMARK
   2/6 < 5/8

4. Change one denominator to match the other denominator

    3/4 and 6/12

    3/4 = 9/12

    9/12 > 6/12

5. Find a common denominator.

    2/4 and 3/5

    10/20 and 12/20

    10/20 < 12/20

Adding Fractions

When teaching students to add fractions students should experience it concretely, pictorially, and then abstractly. A great way to start with this is by using area models such as pattern blocks and fraction circles and squares. Then, give students several opportunities to prove their thinking with mathematical sketches. Remember that students use prior experiences with manipulatives to base their sketches on. After the students know how to illustrate their thinking, they should then learn how to order and compare fractions based on reasoning (see Figures 8.17, 8.18, 8.19, and 8.20).

Concept: Building an understanding of adding fractions.
Workstations: Adding fractions.

Figure 8.17

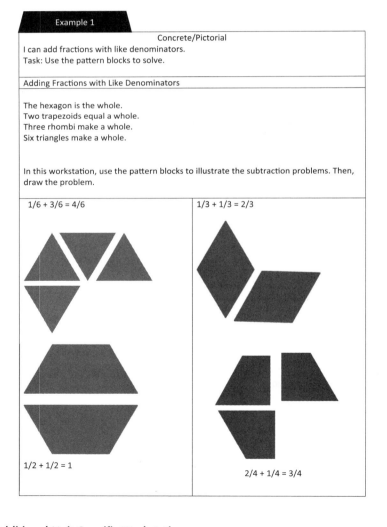

Example 1
Concrete/Pictorial
I can add fractions with like denominators. Task: Use the pattern blocks to solve.
Adding Fractions with Like Denominators
The hexagon is the whole. Two trapezoids equal a whole. Three rhombi make a whole. Six triangles make a whole. In this workstation, use the pattern blocks to illustrate the subtraction problems. Then, draw the problem.

1/6 + 3/6 = 4/6

1/3 + 1/3 = 2/3

1/2 + 1/2 = 1

2/4 + 1/4 = 3/4

Figure 8.18

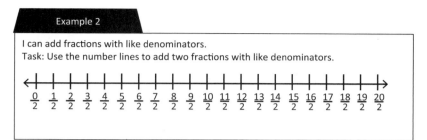

Example 2

I can add fractions with like denominators.
Task: Use the number lines to add two fractions with like denominators.

$$\frac{0}{2} \quad \frac{1}{2} \quad \frac{2}{2} \quad \frac{3}{2} \quad \frac{4}{2} \quad \frac{5}{2} \quad \frac{6}{2} \quad \frac{7}{2} \quad \frac{8}{2} \quad \frac{9}{2} \quad \frac{10}{2} \quad \frac{11}{2} \quad \frac{12}{2} \quad \frac{13}{2} \quad \frac{14}{2} \quad \frac{15}{2} \quad \frac{16}{2} \quad \frac{17}{2} \quad \frac{18}{2} \quad \frac{19}{2} \quad \frac{20}{2}$$

Figure 8.19

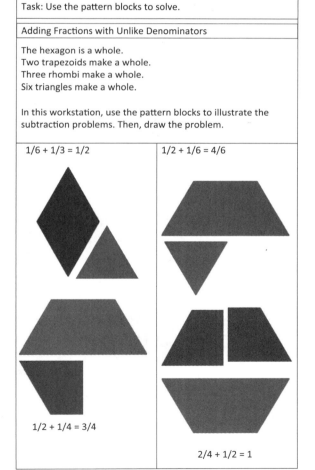

Example 3

Concrete/Pictorial
I can add fractions with unlike denominators. Task: Use the pattern blocks to solve.
Adding Fractions with Unlike Denominators
The hexagon is a whole. Two trapezoids make a whole. Three rhombi make a whole. Six triangles make a whole. In this workstation, use the pattern blocks to illustrate the subtraction problems. Then, draw the problem.

1/6 + 1/3 = 1/2	1/2 + 1/6 = 4/6
1/2 + 1/4 = 3/4	2/4 + 1/2 = 1

Figure 8.20

Example 4

I can add fractions with like denominators.
Task: Pick 2 cards. Add them together.

4/6		5/6

Record your thinking.

Subtracting Fractions

Subtracting fractions should also parallel the teaching of adding fractions. Students should be allowed to go through the cycle of engagement, working with concrete materials, sketching, and then just numbers. They should also be required to learn to represent subtraction of fractions with various tools to illustrate area models, set models, and linear models (see Figure 8.21, 8.22, and 8.23).

Subtracting Fractions

Concept: Building an understanding of subtracting fractions.
Workstations: Subtracting fractions.

Figure 8.21

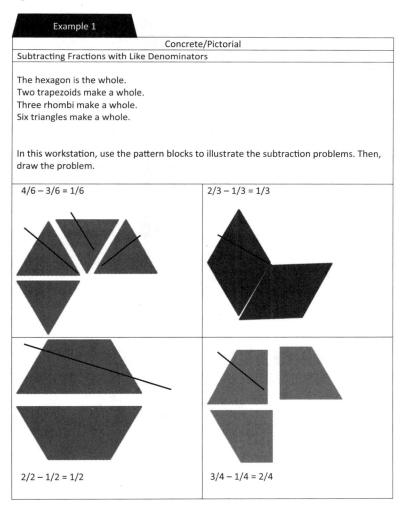

Example 1	
Concrete/Pictorial	
Subtracting Fractions with Like Denominators	
The hexagon is the whole. Two trapezoids make a whole. Three rhombi make a whole. Six triangles make a whole. In this workstation, use the pattern blocks to illustrate the subtraction problems. Then, draw the problem.	
4/6 – 3/6 = 1/6	2/3 – 1/3 = 1/3
2/2 – 1/2 = 1/2	3/4 – 1/4 = 2/4

Figure 8.22

Example 2

Concrete/Pictorial
Subtracting Fractions with Unlike Denominators

The hexagon is the whole.
Two trapezoids make a whole.
Three rhombi make a whole.
Six triangles make a whole.

In this workstation, use the pattern blocks to illustrate the subtraction problems. Then, draw the problem.

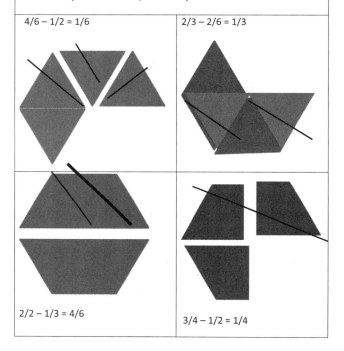

$4/6 - 1/2 = 1/6$	$2/3 - 2/6 = 1/3$
$2/2 - 1/3 = 4/6$	$3/4 - 1/2 = 1/4$

Figure 8.23

Example 3

Abstract
I can subtract fractions with unlike denominators by making equivalent fractions.

Task: Pick a card and subtract the fractions. Use the strategy of making equivalent fractions.

$1/2 - 1/4 =$

$2/4 - 1/4 = 1/4$

Multiplication of Fractions

It is really important to scaffold the teaching of fractions. Workstations should be a reflection of that. If students cannot fluently add and subtract fractions using concrete materials, sketches, and just the numbers then they shouldn't be working on multiplying fractions. Prior knowledge matters. In preparing the fraction workstation level the activities. Don't rush to things that students aren't ready for. Because then they keep going on to the next topic without ever really solidifying any knowledge. The workstation allows the student the space to get good at what they are learning and build on prior knowledge. So, when teaching multiplication of fractions, students will continue learning using a cycle of engagement based on concrete, pictorial, and then abstract experiences based on the area, set, and linear models (see Figures 8.24, 8.25, 8.26, and 8.27).

Multiplying Fractions

Concept: Building an understanding of multiplying fractions.
Workstations: Multiplying fractions.

Figure 8.24

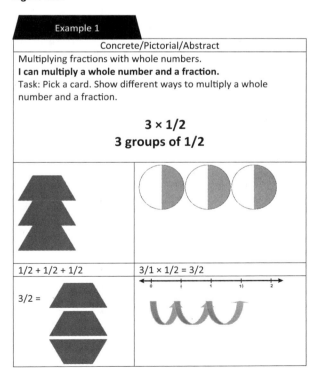

Figure 8.25

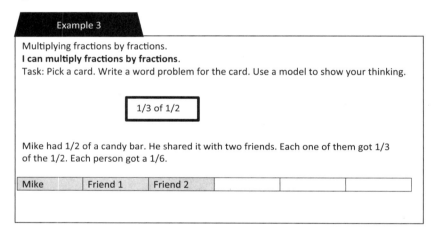

Example 2

Concrete/Pictorial/Abstract

Multiplying fractions by fractions.
I can multiply fractions by fractions.
Task: Pick a card. Show different ways to multiply the fractions.

1/2 × 1/2
A half of a half

1/2 × 1/2 = 1/4

Figure 8.26

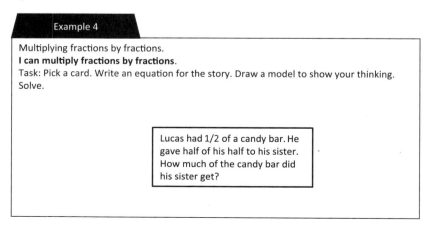

Example 3

Multiplying fractions by fractions.
I can multiply fractions by fractions.
Task: Pick a card. Write a word problem for the card. Use a model to show your thinking.

1/3 of 1/2

Mike had 1/2 of a candy bar. He shared it with two friends. Each one of them got 1/3 of the 1/2. Each person got a 1/6.

Mike		Friend 1	Friend 2			

Figure 8.27

Example 4

Multiplying fractions by fractions.
I can multiply fractions by fractions.
Task: Pick a card. Write an equation for the story. Draw a model to show your thinking. Solve.

Lucas had 1/2 of a candy bar. He gave half of his half to his sister. How much of the candy bar did his sister get?

Dividing Fractions

Last year, I was working with some students. The teacher said that the students completely understood the division of a fraction by a whole number and whole number by a fraction. I always question what the word "knows" means. I find that oftentimes "they know it" means that students know how to procedurally do something. "They know it" doesn't necessarily mean that students fully understand and can explain what they are doing. So, I asked the students to tell me two stories. First, I asked them to tell me a story about dividing 1 by 1/3. They could all do that pretty well. Then I asked them to tell me about 1/3 divided by 2. They had trouble doing that. So, although they could solve both problems procedurally, they couldn't explain what they were doing or even why it worked.

I say this to stress that workstations must allow students to gain a deeper understanding of the concepts that they are working with (see Figures 8.28, 8.29, 8.30, 8.31, 8.32, 8.33, and 8.34). In this workstation, students should have activities where they have to match the story with the equations, where they have to match models with stories, and where they have to write stories about different equations.

Dividing Fractions

Concept: Building an understanding of dividing fractions.
Workstations: Dividing fractions.

Figure 8.28

Example 1
Dividing a whole number by a fraction. **I can divide whole numbers by a fraction.** Task: Pick a card. Write a word problem for the card. Use a model to show your thinking.

$$4 \div 1/2$$

Figure 8.29

Example 2

Dividing fractions with whole numbers.
I can divide whole numbers by fractions.
Task: Pick a card. Write an equation for the story. Draw a model to show your thinking.

> Grandma made three dollars. She gave her granddaughter 1/2 of the money. How much money did she give her granddaughter?

Figure 8.30

Example 3

Dividing fractions with whole numbers.
I can divide whole numbers by fractions.
Task: Match the equations and the stories.

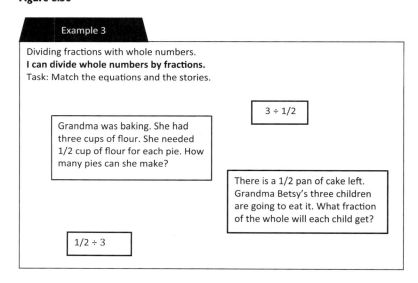

> Grandma was baking. She had three cups of flour. She needed 1/2 cup of flour for each pie. How many pies can she make?

> 3 ÷ 1/2

> There is a 1/2 pan of cake left. Grandma Betsy's three children are going to eat it. What fraction of the whole will each child get?

> 1/2 ÷ 3

Figure 8.31

Example 4

Concrete/Pictorial/Abstract

I can divide a fraction by a whole number.
Task: Pick a card. Show different ways to divide the fraction by the whole number.

$1/2 \div 3$
If you are going to share 1/2 a cookie with three people equally,
how much would each person get?

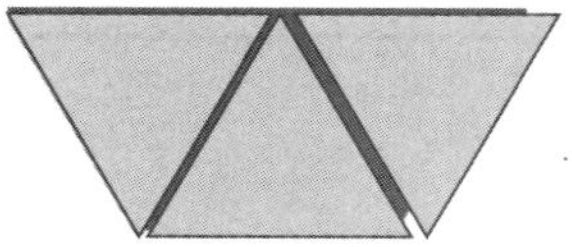

1/6	1/6	1/6	1/6	1/6	1/6

1/6	1/6	1/6
1/6	1/6	1/6

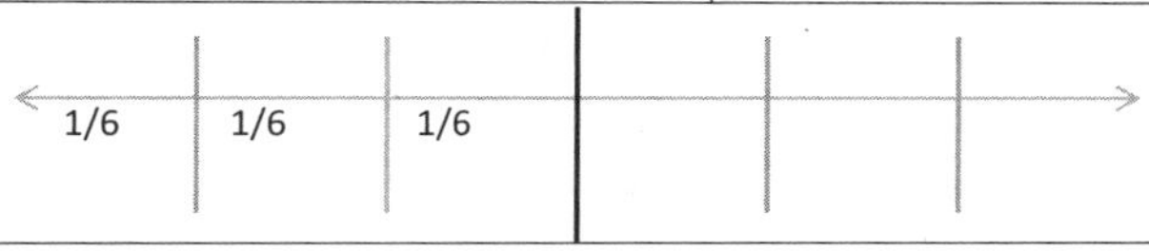 1/6	1/6	1/6

Figure 8.32

Example 5

Dividing a fraction by a whole number.
I can divide a fraction by a whole number.
Task: Pick a card. Write a word problem for the card. Use a model to show your thinking.

$1/2 \div 3$

Figure 8.33

Dividing fractions with whole numbers.
I can divide a fraction by a whole number.
Task: Pick a card. Write an equation for the story. Draw a model to show your thinking.

> Grandma Grace divided her garden in half. She planted all vegetables on one side and all fruit on the other. On the vegetable side, she planted equal amounts of corn, squash, and potatoes. What part of the total garden was corn?

Figure 8.34

Example 7

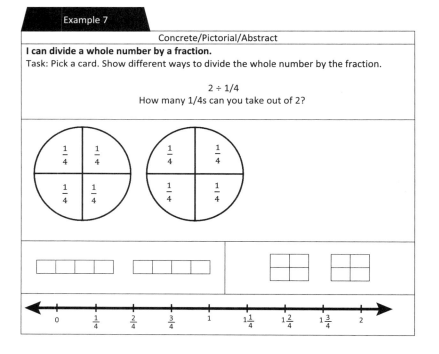

Concrete/Pictorial/Abstract

I can divide a whole number by a fraction.
Task: Pick a card. Show different ways to divide the whole number by the fraction.

2 ÷ 1/4
How many 1/4s can you take out of 2?

Culminating Activities

Culminating activities are important in every unit of study. Choice boards, *Find Someone Who,* and true or false sorts allow students to review the topics. Here are some ideas for a fraction unit (see Figures 8.35, 8.36, 8.37, and 8.38).

Figure 8.35

Choice Board		
You must choose two things from the board to do by the end of the unit. You can work on these projects in your workstations and at home. Please submit your plan to Ms. Thomas by next Wednesday, February 18th. Be sure to look at the specific rubric for your projects.		
Make a poster about fractions.	Make a Glog about fractions.	Design your own project about fractions.
Make a board game to practice adding and subtracting fractions.	Write an essay about fractions in real life. Use numbers, words, and pictures.	Make a PowerPoint about adding fractions.
Do the *Find Someone Who Can* board about fractions.	Make a card game to practice multiplying and dividing fractions.	Make a podcast about multiplying fractions.

Figure 8.36

My Plan for Fraction Projects

Week 1:
First, I will work on the poster project. I am going to do this by myself. I will do this in the Vocabulary/Writing workstation.

Week 2:
Then I will work on the card game for multiplying fractions. I will also do this in the fraction workstation. I am going to design the game in a group.

Figure 8.37

Fractions: Find Someone Who Can...		
I understand fractions. I can discuss different fraction topics. Task: During project choice time, take the board and find different people to fill in your board. Each person must sign their name and prove that they can do the task. They can either write it on the board or on another piece of paper. Each person can only answer one time.		
Write down four equivalent fractions. Signature:	Write a fraction multiplication story. Signature:	Write down three fractions that round to 1. Signature:
Add two fractions with unlike denominators. Signature:	Subtract two fractions with unlike denominators. Signature:	Write two fractions in between 1 and 2. Signature:
Plot three fractions on a number line from least to greatest. Signature:	Divide a whole number by a fraction. Signature:	Write three different statements to compare fractions using the symbols >, <, =. Signature:

Figure 8.38

True or False Sort	
I can sort fraction statements. Task: Pick a card. Decide whether or not it is true or false. Sort the facts. Turn them over and verify if you are correct or not.	

$1/2 = 2/4$ $3/4 > 2/12$ $1/2 = 3/6$

True	False

Teaching in the 21st Century

There is a plethora of tools that students can use to understand fractions (see Figure 8.39). Be sure to read the books about fractions and do some of the activities in the books. Teach them some of the songs. Be sure to download the fraction manipulatives (circles, squares, fraction pattern blocks, and bars) and the pattern block paper so they can represent fractions with these tools. Have the students play some of the internet games as well.

Figure 8.39

Resources for Teaching Fractions			
Picture Books	**Videos**	**Virtual Tools**	**Internet Games**
Apple Fractions by Jerry Pallotta *The Hershey's Milk Chocolate Fractions Book* by Jerry Palotta *If You Were a Fraction* by Trisha Speed Shaskan *Working with Fractions* by David A. Adler *Fraction Action* by Loreen Leedy	https://www.brainpop.com/math/numbersanddoperations/fractions/ http://www.mathplayground.com/howto_comparefractions.html http://pbskids.org/cyberchase/find-it/fractions/	http://illuminations.nctm.org/activity.aspx?id=3577 http://www.glencoe.com/sites/common_assets/mathematics/ebook_assets/vmf/VMF-Interface.html (see bears in a boat for teaching the set model) http://nlvm.usu.edu/en/nav/frames_asid_274_g_2_t_1.html?open=activities Fraction circles: http://www.cehd.umn.edu/ci/rationalnumberproject/flash/circles.swf Cuisenaire Rod™-like blocks: http://www.mathplayground.com/mathbars.html	http://www.mathplayground.com/index_fractions.html http://jmathpage.com/topics/jmpheadfractions.html http://illuminations.nctm.org/activity.aspx?id=4148

Key Points

- Hands-on activities
- Variety of fraction tools
- Virtual fraction tools
- Real-life things
- Games

Summary

Fractions are one of the most difficult topics for students. One of the main goals of the teacher is to get the student on friendly terms with fractions. The way to do that effectively is over time with engaging activities. Students should work with fractions every week of the school year, through energizers and routines so that when they get to their actual unit of study, they are ready. If they do this, they will be completely and totally ready for all the new knowledge because they have practiced all the old knowledge.

Reflection Questions

1. How much of your activities are hands-on versus paper and pencil?
2. In what ways do you have your students make connections to real life?
3. In what ways do you reinforce all of the different vocabulary associated with fractions?

9

Decimal Workstations

The only way to learn mathematics is to do mathematics.
—Paul Halmos[1]

Big Ideas

Decimals are part of our everyday lives, including sports, food, and gas. We use them to represent numbers that are less than one whole.

Enduring Understandings

- There are many different ways to represent decimals.
- Decimals are part of the base ten system.
- Decimal is another name for a fraction and can be found in the same place on the number line.
- Patterns can be seen when multiplying numbers by powers of ten.

What it Means for a Workstation

The goal of the decimal workstation is for students to understand what decimals are and how we use them in everyday life. We need to use different types of models of real-life situations so that students understand the use of decimals in real life. Students should be able to make everyday connections to the math they are studying. Students need to understand decimals beyond money.

They encounter decimals in their everyday lives. We must help them to make this connection. One day I was in a school in the south Bronx and I walked into a classroom. The teacher had just started to teach decimals. He had put up a textbook problem involving knitting. He looked relieved that I popped in and he asked me if I wanted to take over. I said yes, but I was going to use a different problem.

I began to ask the students about their daily comings and goings to and from the corner bodega (small grocery store). I asked the students if they went into the store and had 50 cents how many bags of potato chips could they buy? Everyone answered two because the chips cost 25 cents each. I then asked if they had 70 cents to share among three people, how much would each person get? They quickly noted 23 cents each with a penny left over. I said okay, if you wanted to buy the lollipops dipped in chili (everyone knew they cost 15 cents), how many could each person buy? They quickly calculated 4.

We continued with this line of thought for several minutes. Then, I told the 5th graders that we had just been practicing dividing decimals. I asked them to share their strategies (which varied). After we discussed it and practiced a few more problems, the teacher then introduced the traditional algorithm. The students got it because they understood it. Personally, if we hadn't been rushed by the pacing calendar, I wouldn't have introduced the algorithm that same day. I would let the students play around and make up their own problems and solutions for a few days before rushing to the abstract. To even my surprise though, most of the exit slips said "dividing decimals is easy." This was a great start to a good unit!

This is the way we need to teach decimals (really all math in general). Making connections to students' lives not only makes sense, but it makes all the difference. Students understand what they do every day. When we can "mathematize" it, they "get it." They get it because they live it. So, the workstations should capitalize on this fact. When teaching decimals, go and round up the circulars of the local neighborhood hotspots—the delis, the grocery stores, the drugstores, the restaurants, and the fast food joints. Anywhere where students spend time. Get those things and let those real-life things launch your lessons.

Decimal Anchor Charts

Anchor charts are essential. So many different issues can be addressed with anchor charts. When you put QR codes on them, they become truly "smart charts" that help students see and visualize and think about the concepts.

Anchor charts should talk about the concept, skills, and connections to everyday life (see Figures 9.1, 9.2, 9.3, 9.4, 9.5, and 9.6).

Figure 9.1

WHAT IS A DECIMAL?

A decimal is a part of a whole. For example , a dime is a tenth of a dollar.

Figure 9.2

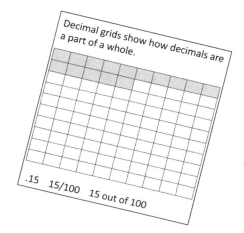

Decimal grids show how decimals are a part of a whole.

.15   15/100   15 out of 100

Figure 9.3

WHAT WORDS DO WE USE TO DESCRIBE DECIMALS?

Tenths : .10

Hundredths : .01

Thousandths : .001

Figure 9.4

HOW DO WE USE DECIMALS IN REAL LIFE?

Money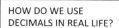
For example, the oranges cost $1.10 a pound.
Sports
Phelps finished in 1.54...

Figure 9.5

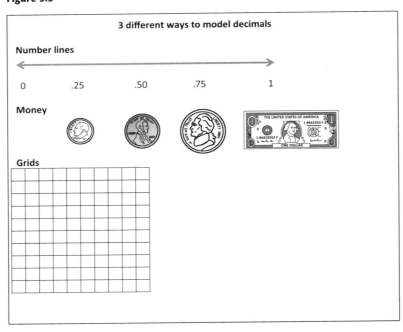

Figure 9.6

How do you use decimals in your everyday life?

Money Buying food, buying candy
Time Getting up, time in school, time at home, TV, dance or sport practice, going to bed
Sports Timeframes in many sports activities are calculated in decimals
Weight Many foods are weighed

Figure 9.7

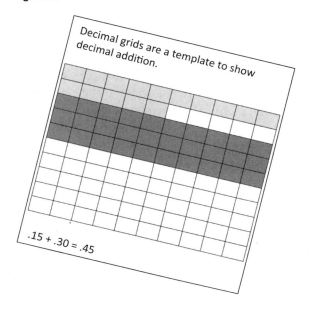

Decimal grids are a template to show decimal addition.

.15 + .30 = .45

Language Frames

Language frames help students talk about the concepts they are learning. Be sure that students have them in their workstations to help scaffold the discussions between them (see Figures 9.8 and 9.9).

Figure 9.8

3/10 is equivalent to 30/100.

Figure 9.9

Expanded notation example
We can say that 3/10 in expanded form is 3 × 1/10.

Decimal Toolkits

The Classroom as a Group Toolkit

The classroom is the first toolkit. Everything in it should teach. Everything that the students have in their decimal toolkits, the teacher should have a large version of in the classroom. These tools are what students use to think through and make sense of the concepts.

Decimal Bars

Decimal bars are important because they scaffold thinking about decimals being numbers on a number line. They are great because students can cut apart a set (laminated on a tag) so that they can use them concretely. They are also great because you can have them on paper in black and white (either laminated or in a sheet protector) so that students can use them to think about their ideas pictorially and shade them to help with comparisons and operations. Each line represents a different decimal. This builds on the model of using fraction bars so many students can easily make the transition of using them (see Figure 9.10).

Figure 9.10

Decimal Bars											
1											
0.50						0.50					
0.33				0.33				0.33			
0.25			0.25			0.25			0.25		
0.20		0.20		0.20		0.20			0.20		
0.166		0.166		0.166		0.166		0.166		.166	
0.125		0.125	0.125		0.125		0.125	0.125		0.125	
0.10	0.10	0.10	0.10	0.10	0.10	0.10	0.10	0.10	0.10		
.083	.083	.083	.083	.083	.083	.083	.083	.083	.083	.083	.083

Number Lines

Every classroom where decimals are taught should have a decimal number line in it. The decimal number lines should be visual. There are a few different ways to represent the decimal number line. One way is to have students create a visual decimal number line by lining the decimal grids together (see Figure 9.11). So, this would look like:

Figure 9.11

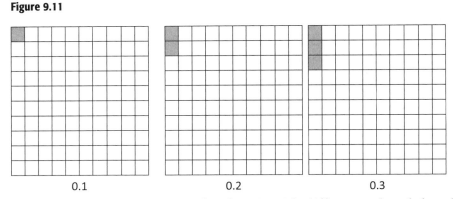

0.1   0.2   0.3

Another way to create a number line is with different colored decades (see Figure 9.12).

Figure 9.12

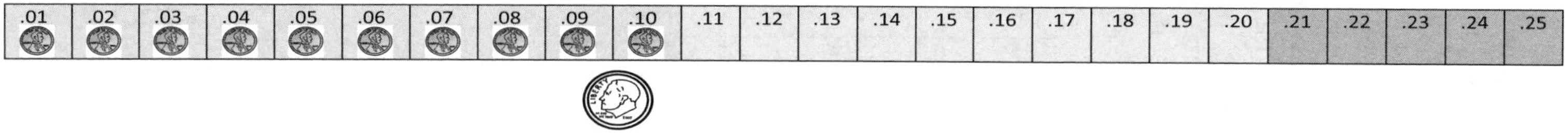

Another way is to have a decimal line with tenths and/or the fractions underneath. It is a good idea to have one of the lines have the decimal fractions visible on the same line so that students are constantly seeing the connection.

Decimal Mat

The decimal mat is becoming increasingly popular. I have even seen them now on popular classroom posters hanging just like hundreds grids (see Figure 9.13). This should be hung up and laminated so that students can go up to the board and think about them. They should also have them in their toolkits so they can use them to reason about decimals.

Figure 9.13

0.01	0.02	0.03	0.04	0.05	0.06	0.07	0.08	0.09	0.1
0.11	0.12	0.13	0.14	0.15	0.16	0.17	0.18	0.19	0.2
0.21	0.22	0.23	0.24	0.25	0.26	0.27	0.28	0.29	0.3
0.31	0.32	0.33	0.34	0.35	0.36	0.37	0.38	0.39	0.4
0.41	0.42	0.43	0.44	0.45	0.46	0.47	0.48	0.49	0.5
0.51	0.52	0.53	0.54	0.55	0.56	0.57	0.58	0.59	0.6
0.61	0.62	0.63	0.64	0.65	0.66	0.67	0.68	0.69	0.7
0.71	0.72	0.73	0.74	0.75	0.76	0.77	0.78	0.79	0.8
0.81	0.82	0.83	0.84	0.85	0.86	0.87	0.88	0.89	0.9
0.91	0.92	0.93	0.94	0.95	0.96	0.97	0.98	0.99	1

Decimal Grids

One of the best manipulatives for teaching decimals is the area model. Many people use base ten blocks to teach decimals. Although this is common, it isn't preferable because most of the time students have already been using base ten blocks as whole numbers. So, to have them switch their thinking to base ten blocks as decimals is difficult. Thinking about them with a completely different tool gives the students a fresh slate. Decimal grids are great because they are a different tool, unlike base ten blocks the model shows the whole (uncut) then the tenths, then the hundredths and thousandths (see Figures 9.14 and 9.15).

Figure 9.14

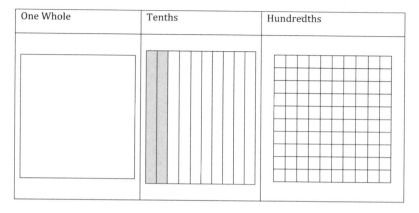

One Whole	Tenths	Hundredths

Figure 9.15

Decimal Squares

These are great manipulatives created by Albert B. Bennet, Jr. He has hands-on manipulatives, books, and interactive games. Check them out at http://www.decimalsquares.com/.

Place Value Chart

A place value chart is important because it allows students to see the whole picture. They can begin to reason about the relative size of numbers. We tend to rush students to work with larger numbers and reason about them when they don't really understand them. We should spend a great deal of time in workstations building understanding with models (see Figure 9.16).

Figure 9.16

Billions	Hundred-millions	Ten-millions	Millions	Hundred-thousands	Thousands	Tens	Ones	.	Tenths	Hundredths	Thousandths

Decimal Wheel

Decimal wheels are great! They help students to visualize decimals as well (see Figure 9.17).

Figure 9.17

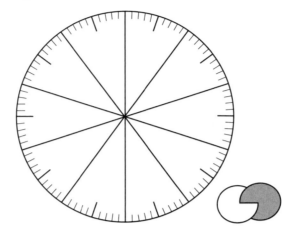

Money Model

We should definitely have money models of decimals up on the wall. This is one of the greatest connections that students can make about decimals (see Figure 9.18).

Figure 9.18

Decimals are a part of a whole.

In real life we use decimals every day. We use money.

A dollar is one whole.

A dime is one-tenth of a dollar.

A nickel is five-hundredths of a dollar.

Pennies are one-hundredth of a dollar.

Activities for Building Understanding

Representing Decimals

In the beginning of the decimal unit it is important to spend a great deal of time on the models. Students should learn a variety of models and use them with the appropriate contexts. Have the students represent, order, and compare decimals with these models to demonstrate a thorough knowledge of the concept.

Concept: Building an understanding of the concept of a decimal.
Workstation: Represent a decimal in many ways.

Figure 9.19

Example 1	
I know and I am able to use numerals, words, and illustrations to discuss decimals. Task: Write the decimal: .25	
Word form Twenty -five hundredths	Fraction form 25/100
Expanded form .20 + .05	Expanded notation $2 \times 1/10 + 5 \times 1/100$
Compose it in two ways .05 + .05 + .05 + .05 + 05 .10 + .10 + .05	Model it on a decimal grid

Figure 9.20

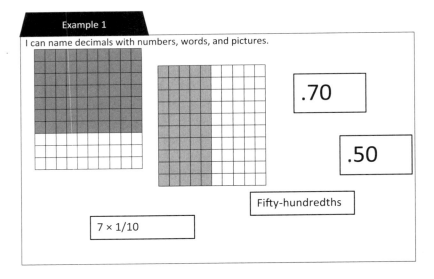

Example 1

I can name decimals with numbers, words, and pictures.

.70

.50

Fifty-hundredths

7 × 1/10

Figure 9.21

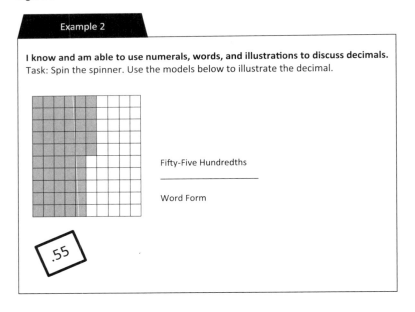

Example 2

I know and am able to use numerals, words, and illustrations to discuss decimals.
Task: Spin the spinner. Use the models below to illustrate the decimal.

Fifty-Five Hundredths

_____

Word Form

.55

Figure 9.22

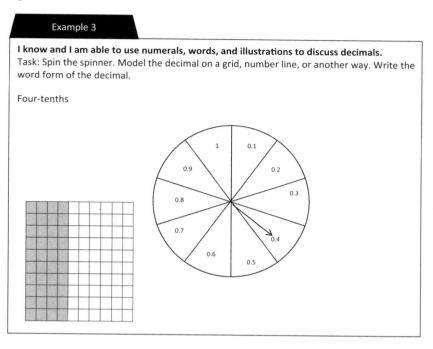

Example 3

I know and I am able to use numerals, words, and illustrations to discuss decimals.
Task: Spin the spinner. Model the decimal on a grid, number line, or another way. Write the word form of the decimal.

Four-tenths

Figure 9.23

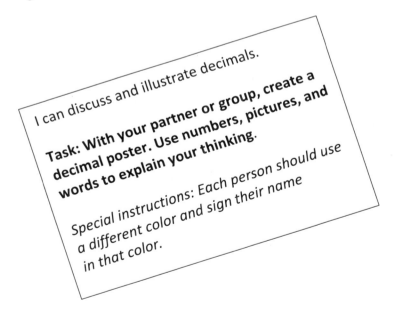

I can discuss and illustrate decimals.

Task: With your partner or group, create a decimal poster. Use numbers, pictures, and words to explain your thinking.

Special instructions: Each person should use a different color and sign their name in that color.

Figure 9.24

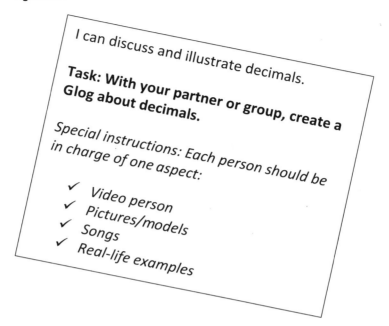

I can discuss and illustrate decimals.

Task: With your partner or group, create a Glog about decimals.

Special instructions: Each person should be in charge of one aspect:

- ✓ Video person
- ✓ Pictures/models
- ✓ Songs
- ✓ Real-life examples

Figure 9.25

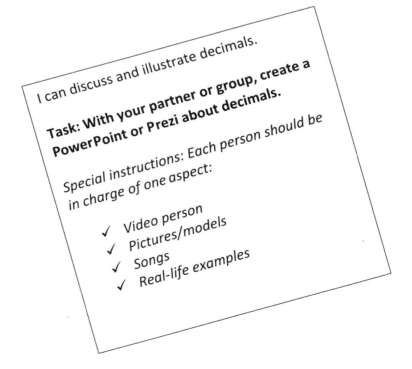

I can discuss and illustrate decimals.

Task: With your partner or group, create a PowerPoint or Prezi about decimals.

Special instructions: Each person should be in charge of one aspect:

- ✓ Video person
- ✓ Pictures/models
- ✓ Songs
- ✓ Real-life examples

Ordering and Comparing Decimals

There should definitely be a system for students to order and compare decimals (see Figures 9.26, 9.27, and 9.28). Have a number line hanging up in the classroom at all times for general reference. Have a number line that students can walk on at all times for general reference. Remember that the research shows that students should see a visual representation on the number line. Students should also have a marked and an unmarked number line in their toolkits.

Ordering Decimals

Concept: Ordering decimals.
Workstation: Ordering decimals on a number line.

Figure 9.26

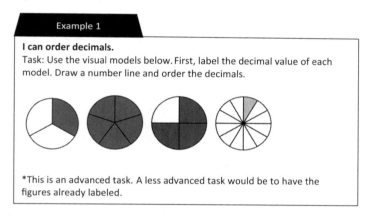

Figure 9.27

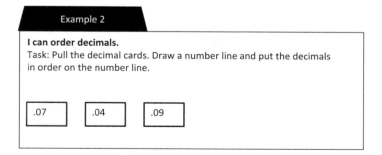

Figure 9.28

> **Example 3**
>
> **I can order decimals.**
> Task: Roll the dice five times. The green dice is the tenths and the yellow dice is the hundredths. Draw a number line and put the decimals in order on the number line.
>
> ←——————————————————————————→

Comparing Decimals

Concept: Comparing decimals (see Figures 9.29, 9.30, 9.31, and 9.32).
Workstation: Comparing decimals concretely, pictorially, and abstractly.

Figure 9.29

> **Example 1**
>
> **I can compare decimals using visual models.**
> Task 1: Pull four different decimal circle cards. Compare the decimals using the symbols = ,<, >. Write four different statements.

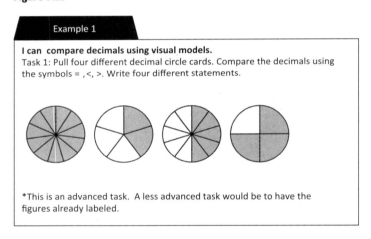

> *This is an advanced task. A less advanced task would be to have the figures already labeled.

Figure 9.30

> **Example 2**
>
> **I can compare decimals using visual models.**
> Pick two cards. Compare decimals using the decimal bars.

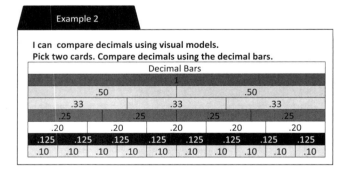

Figure 9.31

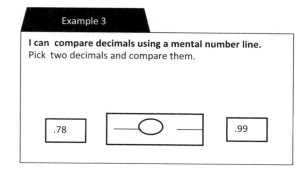

Example 3

I can compare decimals using a mental number line.
Pick two decimals and compare them.

.78   .99

Figure 9.32

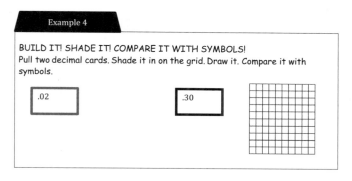

Example 4

BUILD IT! SHADE IT! COMPARE IT WITH SYMBOLS!
Pull two decimal cards. Shade it in on the grid. Draw it. Compare it with symbols.

.02   .30

Figure 9.33

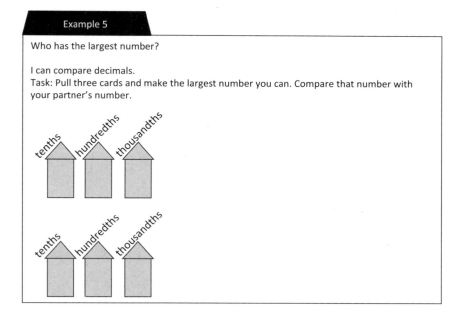

Example 5

Who has the largest number?

I can compare decimals.
Task: Pull three cards and make the largest number you can. Compare that number with your partner's number.

tenths   hundredths   thousandths

tenths   hundredths   thousandths

Reasoning About Decimals

Give students many opportunities to refer to their number line and reason about numbers. At first, let the students refer to the number line as they are doing it. Then later on let them do it and only refer to the number line to double check. Also, use a variety of number generators, such as cards, dice, and spinners.

Concept: Decimals on a number line (see Figures 9.34 and 9.35).
Workstation: Reasoning about decimals.

Figure 9.34

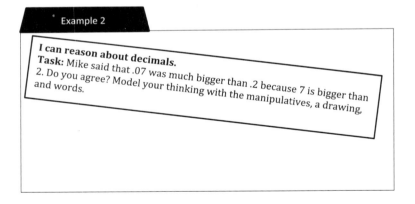

Example 1

Reasoning About Decimals

I can reason about decimals.
Task: Pick a decimal card and write the decimal in the correct column.

Less than .50	Near .50	Near 1	More than 1
.42	.67	.95	1.25

Figure 9.35

Example 2

I can reason about decimals.
Task: Mike said that .07 was much bigger than .2 because 7 is bigger than 2. Do you agree? Model your thinking with the manipulatives, a drawing, and words.

Composing and Decomposing Decimals

Concept: Composing and decomposing decimals (see Figures 9.36, 9.37, 9.38, and 9.39).
Workstation: To put together and break apart decimals in a variety of ways.

Figure 9.36

Example 1

I can compose decimals.

Task: Pull a card or roll the dice. Show two ways to make the decimal.

.57

Way 1: .50 + .07   Way 2: .10 + .47

Figure 9.37

Example 2

I can compose decimals.

Task: Show three ways to compose .20. Use numbers, pictures , and words.

Figure 9.38

Example 3

Composing a Decimal

Concept: Using a model to compose decimals.
Task: Use money to compose decimals.

Composing a decim al means making it.
Let's take .75.

We can build it many ways.

Way 1:

   = .25 + .25+ .25 = .75

Way 2:

     = .10+.10+.05 + .25+ .25 = .75

Figure 9.39

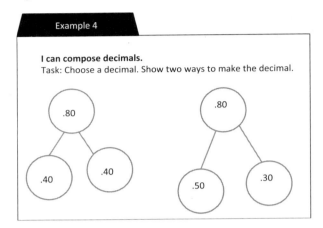

Example 4

I can compose decimals.
Task: Choose a decimal. Show two ways to make the decimal.

.80

.40   .40

.80

.50   .30

Equivalent Decimals

Students should understand through experience that pieces of the whole can be cut up into different amounts and some of those amounts can equal each other (see Figures 9.40, 9.41, 9.42, 9.43, and 9.44). Decimal bars are important in order for students to visualize equivalent decimals. Have students make their own set by paper folding and cutting. Relate this to what they did with the fraction bars.

Concept: Equivalent decimals.
Workstation: To work with equivalent decimals on the concrete, pictorial, and abstract level.

Figure 9.40

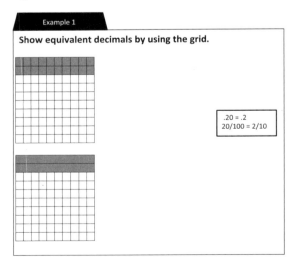

Example 1

Show equivalent decimals by using the grid.

.20 = .2
20/100 = 2/10

Equivalent Decimal Bingo

Figure 9.41

Example 2

I can name equivalent decimals.
Task: Pick a bingo card.
Directions: Have a bingo card caller. The caller flips a bingo card. Everybody looks on their board for an equivalent decimal. Whoever gets three in a row or all four corners first wins.

1/10   .001   1/100   3 × 1/100   2 -thousandths 8-tenths .0700
.057   9/1000

.1	57 × 1/100	.800
.009	.01	.07
1/1000	.03	.002

1/1000	.03	.002
.01	.07	.009
.1	57 × 1/100	.800

.002	.01	.07
.009	.03	.800
1/1000	. 57 × 1/100	.1

.1	.002	1/1000
.01	57 × 1/100	.07
.800	.03	.009

Example 3

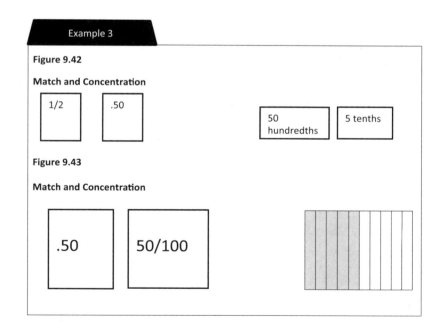

Figure 9.42

Match and Concentration

| 1/2 | | .50 |

| 50 hundredths | | 5 tenths |

Figure 9.43

Match and Concentration

| .50 | | 50/100 |

Figure 9.44

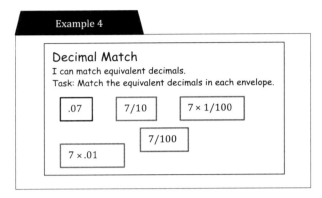

Example 4

Decimal Match
I can match equivalent decimals.
Task: Match the equivalent decimals in each envelope.

| .07 | 7/10 | 7 × 1/100 |

| 7/100 |

| 7 × .01 |

Rounding Decimals

It is important that students understand rounding conceptually by actually looking at how and why we round up or down. Start by having students do rounding with beaded number lines, where there are a hundred beads in groups of ten. The individual beads represent hundredths. In order to teach rounding, the students find the number, for example 34/100, and they see that it is closer to 30/100 than 40/100. They can see it and feel it. Then, they can do this with hundredth grids.

Figure 9.45

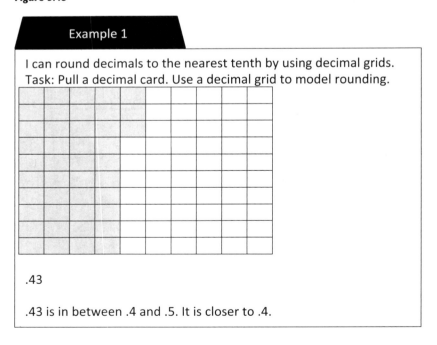

Example 1

I can round decimals to the nearest tenth by using decimal grids.
Task: Pull a decimal card. Use a decimal grid to model rounding.

.43

.43 is in between .4 and .5. It is closer to .4.

Figure 9.46

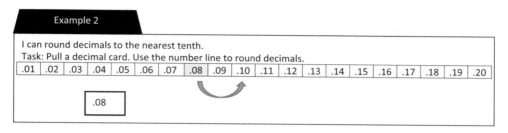

Example 2

I can round decimals to the nearest tenth.
Task: Pull a decimal card. Use the number line to round decimals.

| .01 | .02 | .03 | .04 | .05 | .06 | .07 | .08 | .09 | .10 | .11 | .12 | .13 | .14 | .15 | .16 | .17 | .18 | .19 | .20 |

.08

Figure 9.47

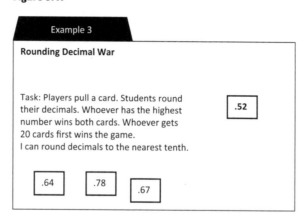

Example 3

Rounding Decimal War

Task: Players pull a card. Students round their decimals. Whoever has the highest number wins both cards. Whoever gets 20 cards first wins the game.
I can round decimals to the nearest tenth.

.52

.64   .78   .67

Decimal Operations

It is essential that students have fluency with addition, subtraction, multiplication, and division of whole numbers before they start to work with decimals, because the same strategies they learned for whole numbers they will be using for decimals. Too often, we rush to decimal operations and students still can't do those same things with whole numbers. You must slow down to speed up. Teach whole numbers well and decimals won't be a problem. There is a strong emphasis in all of the sections below on the modeling of the operation. We want students to conceptually understand what they are doing, be able to illustrate it in different ways, and think flexibly about the numbers.

Adding Decimals

Concept: Adding decimals (Figures 9.48, 9.49, and 9.50).
Workstation: Adding decimals concretely, pictorially and abstractly.

Figure 9.48

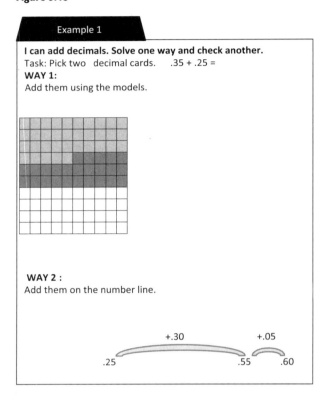

Example 1

I can add decimals. Solve one way and check another.
Task: Pick two decimal cards.   .35 + .25 =
WAY 1:
Add them using the models.

WAY 2 :
Add them on the number line.

+.30   +.05
.25   .55   .60

Figure 9.49

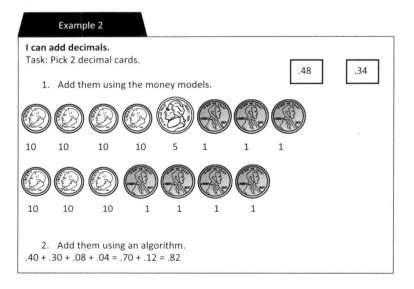

Example 2

I can add decimals.
Task: Pick 2 decimal cards.

.48   .34

1. Add them using the money models.

10   10   10   10   5   1   1   1

10   10   10   1   1   1   1

2. Add them using an algorithm.
.40 + .30 + .08 + .04 = .70 + .12 = .82

Figure 9.50

Example 3

I can add decimals.
Task: Pick two decimal cards. Add them on a number line. Add them using the grids. Add them using another strategy.

.33   .28

Add decimals	Add as fractions
.33 + .28 = .61	33/100 + 28/100 = 31/100 + 30/100 = 61/100
Use grids	Number line
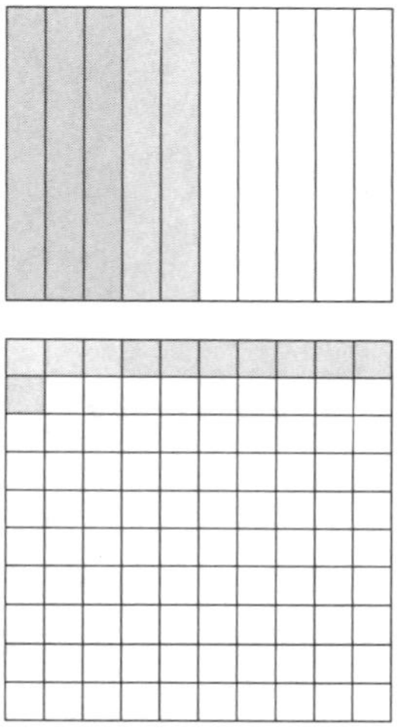	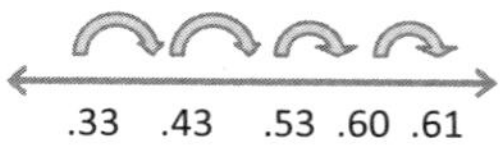 .33 .43 .53 .60 .61

Subtracting Decimals

Concept: Subtracting decimals (Figures 9.51, 9.52, and 9.53).

Figure 9.51

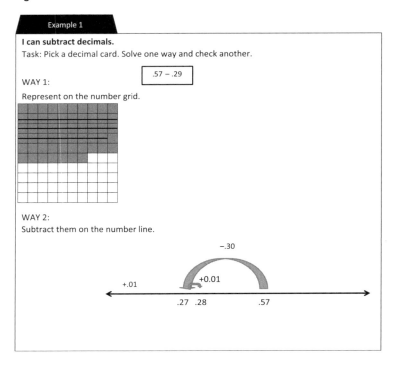

Example 1

I can subtract decimals.
Task: Pick a decimal card. Solve one way and check another.

.57 − .29

WAY 1:
Represent on the number grid.

WAY 2:
Subtract them on the number line.

−.30

+.01   +0.01

.27 .28   .57

Figure 9.52

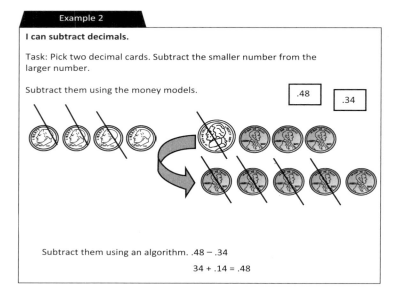

Example 2

I can subtract decimals.

Task: Pick two decimal cards. Subtract the smaller number from the larger number.

Subtract them using the money models.

.48   .34

Subtract them using an algorithm. .48 − .34

34 + .14 = .48

Figure 9.53

Example 3

I can subtract decimals.
Task: Pick two decimal cards. Subtract then on a number line. Subtract them using the grids. Subtract them using a traditional algorithm.

.33   .28

Subtract decimals	Subtract as fractions
.33 – .28 = .05	33/100 – 28/100 = 5/100
Use Grids	**Number line**

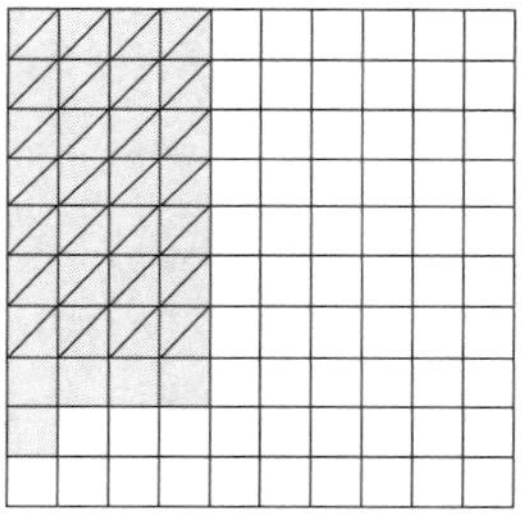

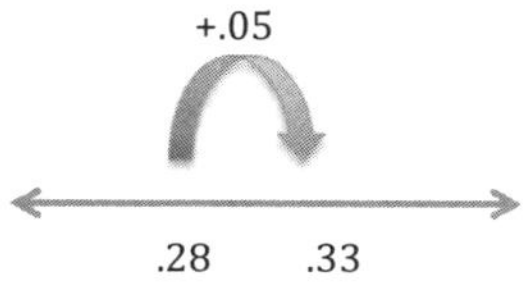

+.05

.28   .33

.28 + .05 = .33

You can count up to find the difference. You could also count back.

Multiplying Decimals

Concept: Multiplying decimals (see Figures 9.54 and 9.55).
Workstation: Multiplying decimals concretely, pictorially, and abstractly.

Figure 9.54

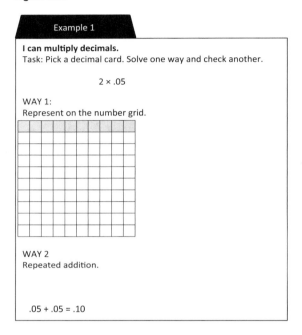

Figure 9.55

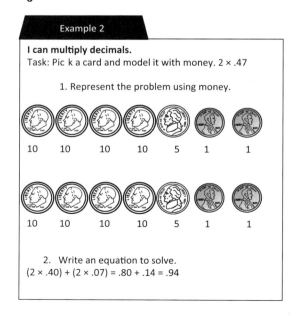

Dividing Decimals

Concept: Dividing decimals (see Figures 9.56, 9.57, and 9.58).
Workstation: Dividing decimals concretely, pictorially, and abstractly.

Figure 9.56

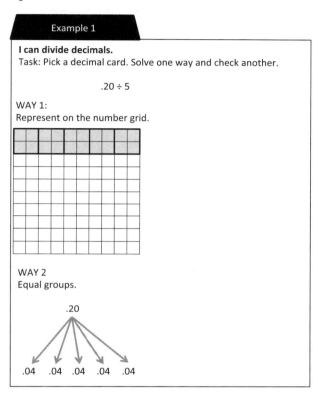

Figure 9.57

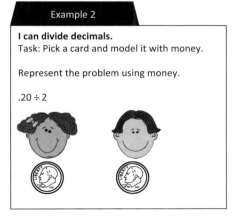

Figure 9.58

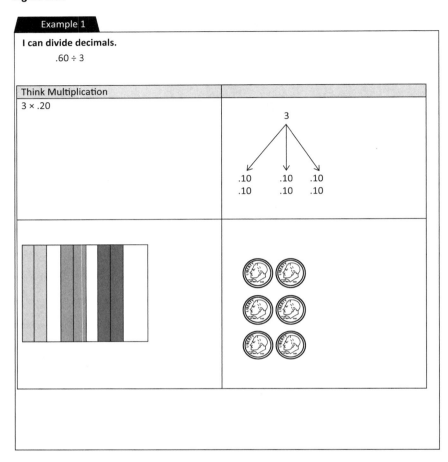

Example 1

I can divide decimals.

.60 ÷ 3

Think Multiplication	
3 × .20	

Building a Productive Disposition

Students should be given the opportunity to reflect on their learning throughout the unit of study (see Figures 9.59 and 9.60).

Figure 9.59

How are you doing with decimals?

What are you doing really well?

What do you still need to work on in this unit?

Figure 9.60

Write a one-minute paper about everything you know about decimals! Use numbers, words, and pictures.

Culminating Activities

At the end of the unit there are different learning structures to help students review and show their understanding of the concepts. Here is an example of what this might look like at the end of a decimal unit.

Choice Boards

It is important to give students choice boards so that they can choose ways to demonstrate their learning of the content. In this particular board, the students have to choose two things, make a plan with some deadlines, and follow the rubrics to complete the plan (see Figures 9.61 and 9.62).

Figure 9.61

Choice Board		
You must choose two things from the board to do by the end of the unit. You can work on these projects in your workstations and at home. Please submit your plan to Ms. Thomas by next Wednesday, February 18th. Be sure to look at the specific rubric for your projects.		
Make a poster about decimals.	Make a Glog about decimals.	Design your own project about decimals.
Make a decimals board game.	Write an essay about different models for decimals. Use numbers, words , and pictures.	Make a PowerPoint about decimals.
Do the Find Someone Who Can board.	Make a card game to practice decimal multiplication and/or division.	Make a podcast about the addition and/or subtraction of decimals.

Figure 9.62

My Plan for the Decimal Projects

Week 1:
First, I will work on the poster project. I am going to do this by myself. I will do this in the Vocabulary/Writing workstation.

Week 2:
Then I will work on a strategy board game. I will also do this in the Fluency workstation. I am going to design the game in a group.

Find Someone Who is more like a group review where several people are involved and everybody is learning (see Figure 9.63a).

Figure 9.63a

Decimal: Find Someone Who...

I understand decimals. I can discuss and explain different strategies.

Task: During project choice time, take the board and find different people to fill in your board. Each person must sign their name and prove that they can do the task. They can either write it on the board or on another piece of paper. Each person can only answer one time.

Multiply decimals using the area model.	Multiply decimals using the open array.	Multiply decimals using money as an example.
Signature:	Signature:	Signature:
Model division of decimals on the number grid.	Model division of decimals using money as an example.	Add decimals by solving one way and checking another.
Signature:	Signature:	Signature:
Subtract decimals by solving one way and checking another.	Write a decimal in both expanded form and expanded notation.	Explain and give two examples of decimals in real life.
Signature:	Signature:	Signature:

True or false sorts allow the students to reason about the learned concepts. These tend to be tricky for students and require that they stop, concentrate, and then make thinking decisions before they choose an answer (see Figure 9.63b).

Figure 9.63b

True or False Sort

I can sort place value statements.
Task: Pick a card. Decide whether or not it is true or false. Sort the facts. Turn them over and verify if you are corrector not.

.92 = (9 × 1/10) + (2 × 1/100)	2.79 > (2 × 10) + (7 × 1/100)

True	False

Teaching in the 21st Century

There is a plethora of tools that students can use to develop understanding of decimals. Be sure to read the books and do some of the activities in the books. Be sure to download the paper manipulatives, hundreds grids, thousands grids, ten thousands grids, number lines, and more. Have the students play some of the internet games as well (see Figure 9.64).

Figure 9.64

Picture Books	Videos/Teacher Resource Books	Virtual Tools	Internet Games
Fractions, Decimals and Percents by David A. Adler and Edward Miller *Little Numbers* by Edward Packard *Piece = Part = Portion: Fractions = Decimals = Percents* by Scott Gifford *Decimals: My Path to Math* by Claire Piddock	Learnzillion.com *Extending Children's Mathematics: Fractions and Decimals* by Susan Empson and Linda Levi *Young Mathematicians at Work: Construction Fractions, Decimals and Percents* by Catherine Fosnot and Maarten Dolk	http://nlvm.usu.edu/en/nav/vlibrary.html	http://www.math-play.com/decimal-math-games.html http://www.mathplayground.com/index_fractions.html http://www.decimalsquares.com/dsGames/

Key Points

Cycle of engagement:

- Concrete
- Pictorial
- Abstract

Summary

Fluency with decimals is really important and students need a great deal of opportunities to practice with a variety of models. There should be activities ranging from concrete, pictorial, and abstract. Students should be able to work with concrete materials as well as draw out/sketch math models. Students have to be able to look at the structure of numbers in a variety of ways and think about efficient ways to operate on those numbers accordingly. It is important that they are able to build on their fluency with whole numbers before they are expected to use those same strategies with decimals.

Reflection Questions

1. What do you currently do in your decimal workstation?
2. Do you have a variety of opportunities for students to practice different strategies?
3. What new ideas do you have from this chapter?
4. What is one change that you will make?

Note

1. http://mathequalslove.blogspot.com/2014/06/more-free-math-and-non-math-quote.html

10

Measurement Workstations

Our students make sense of math when they do math that makes sense.

Big Ideas

Measurement is part of our everyday lives. There are two systems: customary and metric.

Enduring Understandings

- Measurement involves conversions from greater to smaller and smaller to greater.
- Measurement involves area, perimeter, volume, capacity, weight, length, time, money, angles.
- Things can be compared using terms such as greater than, less than and equal to, longer than, shorter than and equal to.
- There are specific tools we use to measure things (like rulers, beakers, tape measures, measuring cups, scales, balances, etc.).

What it Means for a Workstation

The goal of the measurement workstation is for students to get their hands on pounds, kilos, measuring cups, rulers, measuring tapes, and all the tools that students need to actually hold and use to explore measurement. Measurement is often taught through pictures. It should be taught as a VERB. Students should be doing the things they are studying. Teachers should have students pouring liquids when they are looking at capacity. Gallon Man is great but students should be figuring out problems by actually doing them.

Gallon Man can be a great mnemonic device but should not be the primary way that we teach measurement. By the way, Gallon Man has a cousin named Peter Liter who is excellent for teaching students how to make equivalencies as well (http://www.nicadez.com/2012/07/meet-mr-peter-liter.html). But again, students should actually be using milliliters and liters first. This chapter is not meant to be exhaustive but rather to give you a solid idea about the types of activities that should be in the measurement workstation.

Anchor Charts in the Workstation

Anchor charts are important because they help to reinforce ideas and serve as a reference. Language frames that discuss the phrases that are used for particular topics are also good to hang up for all learners (see Figure 10.1, 10.2, and 10.3).

Figure 10.1

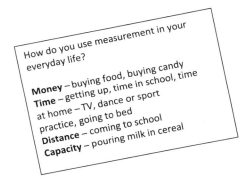

Figure 10.2

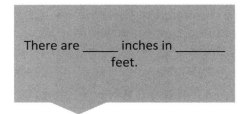

Figure 10.3

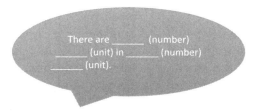

Estimating and Calculating Measurements

Students need opportunities to see, touch, and think about different objects in terms of different measurements. They should be doing activities about:

Length/Distance

- Customary—inches, feet, yards
- Metric—cm, decimeters, meters

Weight

- Customary—oz., lbs.
- Metric—g, kg

Capacity

- Customary—pints, cups, quarts, gallons
- Metric—ml, l, kiloliters

See examples of the estimate/calculating stations below (see Figures 10.4, 10.5, and 10.6).

Concept: Building an understanding of estimating and calculating measurements. Workstation: Estimating and calculating measurements.

Figure 10.4

Example 1			
I can measure using different units.			
Task: Look in the box and pick an item. Estimate the measurement. Then actually check the measurement. Record the information in the chart.			

Estimate and Calculate in Grams/Kilograms	Estimate	Actual Mass	Notes: Were you close or way off?
Name of item			

Another activity that students should do to learn different types of measurement is play match and concentration games. These activities could be in the vocabulary station, in the digital station, or in the unit of study station.

Concept: Building an understanding of the language of measurements.
Workstation: Estimating and calculating measurements.

Figure 10.5

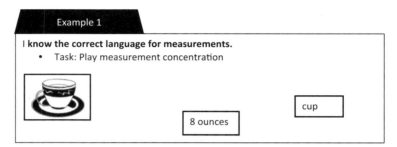

Concept: Building a line plot.
Workstation: Making a line plot.

Figure 10.6

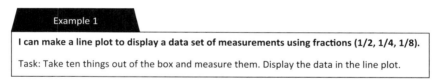

Telling Time and Elapsed Time

Exploring Elapsed Time

Throughout the year, students should practice telling time and elapsed time. I say time because many students are still a little shaky on just telling time, so they need to get strong at that before moving on to telling elapsed time. Provide opportunities for students to review telling time by the hour, half hour, quarter hour, and five-minute and one-minute increments. Give the students a diagnostic that covers all of these elements to see if there are any gaps. Students should play flashcards, bingo, and concentration with both analog and digital time. They should also write stories about time involving real-life scenarios. You should keep time and elapsed time word problems in the word problem workstation throughout the year.

See these sites for ideas:

1. https://www.pinterest.com/drnicki7/telling-time/
2. http://www.sparklebox.co.uk/maths/shape-space-measures/time/#.V_PxsqIrK8U
3. https://www.pinterest.com/search/pins/?q=elapsed%20time%20rulers&rs=typed&term_meta[]=elapsed%7Ctyped&term_meta[]=time%7Ctyped&term_meta[]=rulers%7Ctyped

Money

Money is another important center to have students revisit throughout the year because it is part of our everyday lives. Students struggle with money word problems. Many upper elementary students still have trouble even counting coins. Just like with time, you want to provide review stations as well as grade level stations. Again, give the students a diagnostic to see if there are any gaps in knowledge, understanding, and skills (see Figures 10.7, 10.8, and 10.9).

Figure 10.7

A great picture book launch:

A Quarter from the Tooth Fairy by Caren Holtzman.

After reading this book, have the students explore different ways to make money equivalencies including quarters.

Figure 10.8

Three Must-Have Workstations about Money

https://illuminations.nctm.org/coinbox/

Math Play:
http://www.math-play.com/money-games.html

http://www.mathnook.com/math/skill/countingmoneygames.php

Concept: Building an understanding of money.
Workstations: Working with money.

Figure 10.9

Example 1		
Money Think Dots		
Write a money word problem.	Take one of the restaurant menus and make an order. Calculate your total and what you would get back in change if you gave $20.	Write a 2-step story problem about money.
Make a poster explaining how to count money.	Pick a money word problem from the bag and solve.	Play Kaboom with the money sticks.

Area and Perimeter

Students seem to have more difficulty with calculating perimeter than area. Give them plenty of opportunities to do this. Notice that there are different games, but they all give the students the opportunity to show what they know and not just calculate but also model the concepts (see Figures 10.10, 10.11, 10.12, 10.13, and 10.14).

Concept: Building an understanding of perimeter and area.
Workstations: Estimating and calculating perimeter and area.

Figure 10.10

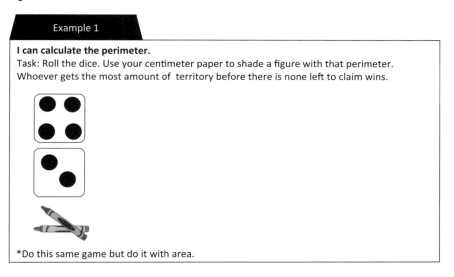

Example 1

I can calculate the perimeter.
Task: Roll the dice. Use your centimeter paper to shade a figure with that perimeter. Whoever gets the most amount of territory before there is none left to claim wins.

*Do this same game but do it with area.

Figure 10.11

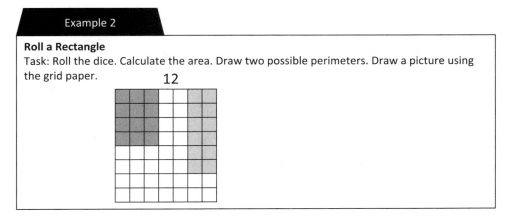

Example 2

Roll a Rectangle
Task: Roll the dice. Calculate the area. Draw two possible perimeters. Draw a picture using the grid paper.

12

Figure 10.12

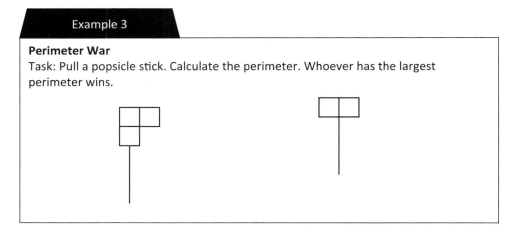

Example 3

Perimeter War

Task: Pull a popsicle stick. Calculate the perimeter. Whoever has the largest perimeter wins.

Figure 10.13

Example 4

Pull a card.	Write two possible equations for the area.	Write two possible equations for the perimeter.	
12			
	1 × 12 = 12	P = 2 (l + w) = 2 (12 + 1) = 26	
	6 × 2 = 12	P = 2 (l + w) = 2 (6 + 2) = 16	

Figure 10.14

Example 5

I can figure out perimeter and area problems.

Task: Choose a card. Take that many one-inch color tiles and paper. Figure out all the ways that you can arrange the tiles.

Measuring Angles

Students should get plenty of opportunities to make angles, paint angles, and find angles in real life. There are plenty of digital games as well as regular games where they can explore and learn the various concepts about angles (see Figures 10.15 and 10.16).

Concept: Building an understanding of estimating and calculating angles.
Workstations: Estimating and calculating angles.

Figure 10.15

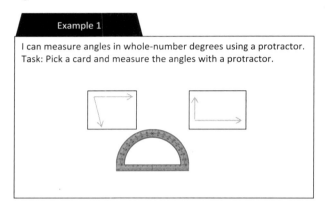

Example 1

I can measure angles in whole-number degrees using a protractor.
Task: Pick a card and measure the angles with a protractor.

Figure 10.16

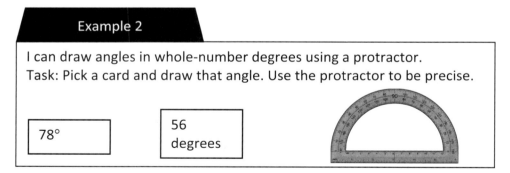

Example 2

I can draw angles in whole-number degrees using a protractor.
Task: Pick a card and draw that angle. Use the protractor to be precise.

78°

56 degrees

*Be sure to have this game as one of the options for learning how to measure angles. It is actually about estimating angles, which is a great skill, but I let the students measure the actual angle. http://www.mathplayground.com/alienangles.html.

Volume

In order to learn about volume, students should be actually doing things to measure it (see Figures 10.17 and 10.18).

Concept: Building an understanding of estimating and calculating volume.
Workstations: Estimating and calculating volume.

Figure 10.17

Example 1

I can calculate the volume of an item.
Task: Determine the volume of the following boxes. Then decide how big the shipping box for ten of these boxes should be. Explain your justification with numbers, words, and pictures.

Box A: Width is 2ft, height is 4ft, length is 5ft
Box B: Width is 5ft, height is 3ft, length is 7ft
Box C: Width is 4ft, height is 4ft, length is 4ft

Figure 10.18

Example 2

Volume War
I can use a formula to calculate the volume of an object.
Task: Calculate the volume on the cards. Then compare with the volume of other players' cards. Whoever has the greatest volume wins. Whoever has the most cards at the end of the game wins.

True or False

True or false sorting games are great ways to get students to reason (see Figure 10.19). This game can be either a culminating activity game or it can be put in the workstation throughout the unit of study about different topics.

Figure 10.19

Example 1

True or False Sort

I can reason about units of measure.

Task: Pick a card. Decide whether or not it is true or false. Sort the facts. Turn them over and verify if you are correct or not.

Pints are larger than quarts	One liter is more liquid than one cup.	A bag of apples is about 3 grams.

True	False

Culminating Activities

There are some generic games that can be tailored to every unit of study that provide engaging purposeful practice with skills and concepts (see Figures 10.20, 10.21, and 10.22).

Figure 10.20

Choice Board		
You must choose two things from the board to do by the end of the unit. You can work on these projects in your workstations and at home. Please submit your plan to Ms. Thomas by next Wednesday, February 18th. Be sure to look at the specific rubric for your projects.		
Make a poster about the metric system.	Make a Glog about the customary system.	Design your own project about measurement.
Make a board game to practice an aspect of measurement.	Write an essay about measurement in real life. Use numbers, words, and pictures.	Make a PowerPoint about measurement.
Do the *Find Someone Who Can* board about measurement.	Make a card game to practice measurement.	Make a podcast about measurement.

Figure 10.21

My Plan for Measurement Projects

Week 1:
First, I will work on the poster project. I am going to do this by myself. I will do this in the Vocabulary/Writing workstation.

Week 2:
Then I will work on the board game about the metric system. I will also do this in the Measurement workstation. I am going to design the game in a group.

Figure 10.22

Measurement: Find Someone Who…		
I understand measurement. I can discuss different units of measure. Task: During project choice time, take the board and find different people to fill in your board. Each person must sign their name and prove that they can do the task. They can either write it on the board or on another piece of paper. Each person can only answer one time.		
Name three different types of units of measure for the metric system. Signature:	Name three different types of units for the customary system. Signature:	Give three real-life examples of things that come in liters and gallons. Signature:
Give three real-life examples of something we measure in grams. Signature:	Discuss the units of measure for length in the metric system. Find some tools to demonstrate in the classroom. Signature:	Discuss the units of measure for weight in the customary system. Use the scale to model your thinking. Signature:
Discuss the units of measure for mass in the metric system. Use the scale to model your thinking. Signature:	Name three foods that you eat and talk about them in terms of their units of measure. Signature:	Choose either the metric system or the customary system and discuss units of measure for capacity. Signature:

Teaching in the 21st Century

There is a plethora of tools that students can use to understand measurement (see Figure 10.23). Be sure to read books about measurement and do some of the activities in the books. Teach them some of the songs. Be sure to download the measurement manipulatives including cubes to measure centimeters, digital rulers, virtual money, clocks, etc. Have the students play some of the internet games as well.

Figure 10.23

Resources for Teaching Measurement		
Picture Books	**Videos/Songs**	**Internet Games**
If you were a Quart or a Liter by Marcie Aboff	Metric System	http://mrnussbaum.com/measurement_games/
If you were a Pound or Kilogram by Marcie Aboff	See the Learn Zillion Measurement Videos by grades https://learnzillion.com	http://www.topmarks.co.uk/maths-games/5-7-years/measures
Inchworm and a Half by Elinor J. Pinczes		http://www.rulergame.net/
Twelve Snails to One Lizard by Susan Hightower	See Songs for Teaching Look up measurement	
How Long and How Wide? by Cecilia Minden	songs by topic http://www.songsforteaching.com/mathsongs.htm	http://www.math-play.com/money-games.html
How Tall, How Short, How Faraway? by David A. Adler		http://www.math-play.com/time-games.html
Measuring Penny by National Geographic Learning		
Counting on Frank by Rod Clement		
The Long and Short of It by Cheryl Nathan		
Millions to Measure by David M. Schwartz		
See Mathstory.com (look up measurement topics such as perimeter, money etc.)		

Key Points

- Hands-on activities
- Real-life things
- Connections to science
- Games

Summary

Measurement is a hands-on endeavor. Students should be working out the problems by using actual things. Students should actually have more of a measurement lab as part of their assessment so that we can check for understanding. We use some type of measurement every day. Students should be making these connections throughout the unit of study and throughout the year.

Reflection Questions

1. Do you allow your students to do the measurement activities?
2. How much of your activities are hands-on versus paper and pencil?
3. In what ways do you have your students make connections to real life?
4. In what ways do you reinforce all of the different vocabulary associated with measurement?

11

Geometry Workstations

> Geometry should be taught in a very concrete and visual manner. "It is surprising how little children learn about shapes from preschool to middle school. . . . We could [and must] do a better job teaching geometry every year."
>
> (Clements and Sarama, 2000, p. 484)

Introduction

Geometry in the elementary grades is so important. The research shows that students need a great deal of hands-on activities so that they can actually experience shapes at the concrete, pictorial, and abstract levels. This chapter is meant to give a few examples that stress the importance of geometry as a kinesthetic and visual undertaking. It is by no means meant to be exhaustive.

Big Ideas (Charles, 2005)

There are shapes and solids. They can be described, classified, and analyzed by their attributes. Orientation and location are important concepts when thinking about shapes. We can transform objects in space in an infinite number of ways and describe and analyze them.

Enduring Understandings (Charles, 2005)

- Points, lines, line segments, and planes are core attributes of space objects.
- Polygons can be described by their sides and angles.
- Polygons can be composed and decomposed into other polygons.

◆ 191

- Triangles and quadrilaterals can be described, categorized, and named based on the relative lengths of their sides and the sizes of their angles. All polyhedrals can be described completely by their faces, edges, and vertices.

Geometry Anchor Charts

Anchor charts serve as a resource for students. Teachers and students should make them. It is also a great learning activity to have students make them in groups and explain them to the class and then display them. (See Figures 11.1, 11.2, and 11.3.)

Figure 11.1

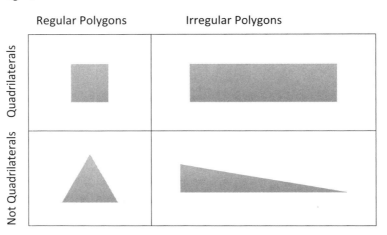

Figure 11.2

Figure 11.3

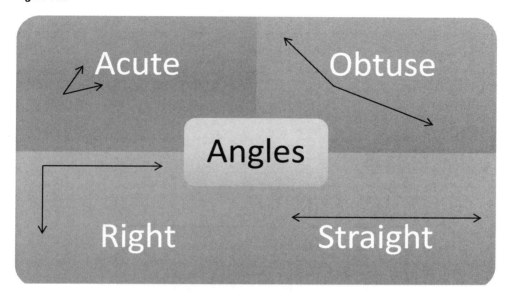

Language Frames

It is important that all students are explicitly taught how to talk in math. Each topic has its own set of words and phrases. It is the responsibility of the teacher to scaffold that language acquisition throughout the unit of study (see Figure 11.4).

Figure 11.4

I can talk about shapes using math words		
Here is an example of a regular polygon...	Here is an example of an irregular polygon...	All shapes are not polygons.

Shapes Workstations

Students should get plenty of opportunities (yes in 3rd, 4th, and 5th grade) to make shapes with Play-Doh, paint them, build them out of craft sticks, and more. These experiences lay the foundation for strong conceptual understanding and the basis for reasoning about shapes and discussing them in complex, sophisticated ways (see Figures 11.5, 11.6, 11.7, 11.8, 11.9, 11.10, and 11.11).

Figure 11.5

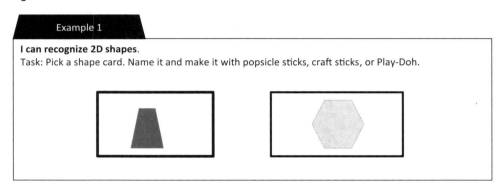

Concept: 2D shapes have specific attributes and properties.
Workstation: Recognize, draw, and build 2D shapes based on their attributes and properties.

Figure 11.6

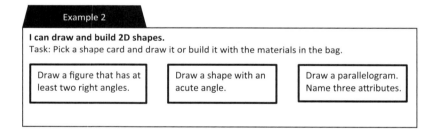

Figure 11.7

Example 3
I can understand that shapes in different categories may share attributes, and that the shared attributes can define a larger category. I can recognize rhombuses, rectangles, and squares as examples of quadrilaterals. Task: Draw a poster that describes quadrilaterals. Task: Draw a poster or create a PowerPoint that describes the similarities and differences between rhombuses, rectangles, and squares.

Figure 11.8

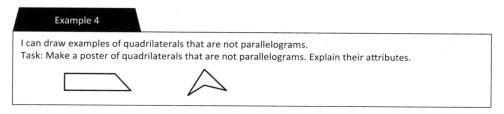

Example 4

I can draw examples of quadrilaterals that are not parallelograms.
Task: Make a poster of quadrilaterals that are not parallelograms. Explain their attributes.

Figure 11.9

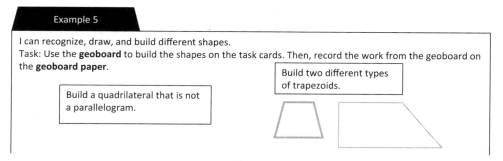

Example 5

I can recognize, draw, and build different shapes.
Task: Use the **geoboard** to build the shapes on the task cards. Then, record the work from the geoboard on the **geoboard paper**.

Build a quadrilateral that is not a parallelogram.

Build two different types of trapezoids.

Students should work with all types of polygons from the beginning. They should discuss regular polygons and irregular polygons.

Figure 11.10

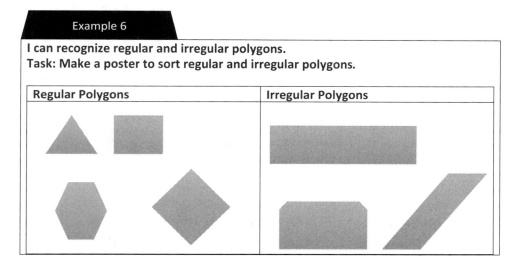

Example 6

I can recognize regular and irregular polygons.
Task: Make a poster to sort regular and irregular polygons.

Regular Polygons	Irregular Polygons

Figure 11.11

Example 7

I can identify and describe shapes.
Task: Fill in the chart with the shape name, definition, and picture

SHAPE NAME	DEFINITION	PICTURE
TRIANGLE	A plane figure with three straight sides and three angles.	
SQUARE	A plane figure with four equal straight sides and four right angles.	
PENTAGON	A plane figure with four straight sides and five angles.	
HEXAGON	A plane figure with six straight sides and six angles.	

It is important to have students work with a variety of materials to explore partitioning shapes into equal parts. I like to use Play-Doh, have students paint shapes and divide them with bingo markers, as well as have students sketch and partition them. It is also important to have students make shapes out of paper and cut them to partition them.

Concept: Shapes can be partitioned into equal parts.
Workstation: To work with shapes concretely, pictorially, and abstractly to show the area of each part of a shape as a unit fraction of the whole.

Figure 11.11a

Example 8

I can partition shapes into equal parts.
Task: Partition different shapes into equal parts.

1/2

Lines and Angles Workstations

Too often, we teach lines by simply looking at them on paper. We must take them off the page and have students discover them in real life: find them, feel them, and build them (see Figures 11.12, 11.13, 11.14, 11.15, 11.16, 11.17, and 11.18).

Concept: Lines and angles have different names and shapes.
Workstation: Recognize, draw, and build different lines and angles.

Figure 11.12

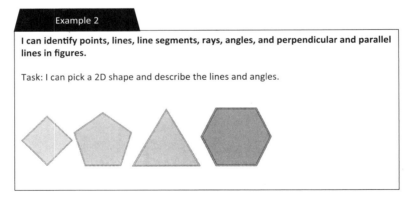

> ### Example 1
>
> **I can identify points, lines, line segments, rays, angles, and perpendicular and parallel lines.**
> Task: Use your straws or pipe cleaners to make a poster of all the different lines.

Figure 11.13

> #### Example 2
>
> **I can identify points, lines, line segments, rays, angles, and perpendicular and parallel lines in figures.**
>
> Task: I can pick a 2D shape and describe the lines and angles.

Figure 11.14

> #### Example 3
>
> **I can identify points, lines, line segments, rays, angles, and perpendicular and parallel lines.**
>
> Task: Make a flipbook that illustrates points, lines, line segments, rays, angles, and perpendicular and parallel lines.

Figure 11.15

Example 4

I can determine the approximate measures of angles in degrees to the nearest whole number using a protractor.

Task: Choose a card and estimate the angle and then measure it.

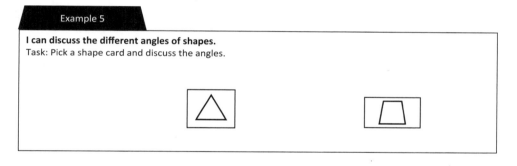

Figure 11.16

Example 5

I can discuss the different angles of shapes.
Task: Pick a shape card and discuss the angles.

Figure 11.17

Example 6

I can determine the measure of an unknown angle formed by two non-overlapping adjacent angles given one or both angle measures.

Task: Pull a card and find the measure of the unknown angle.

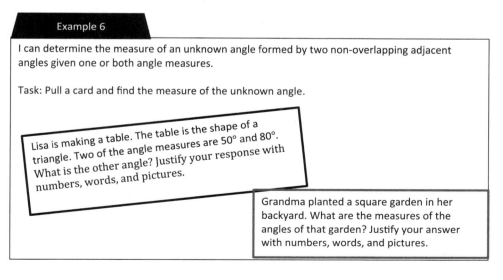

Lisa is making a table. The table is the shape of a triangle. Two of the angle measures are 50° and 80°. What is the other angle? Justify your response with numbers, words, and pictures.

Grandma planted a square garden in her backyard. What are the measures of the angles of that garden? Justify your answer with numbers, words, and pictures.

Figure 11.18

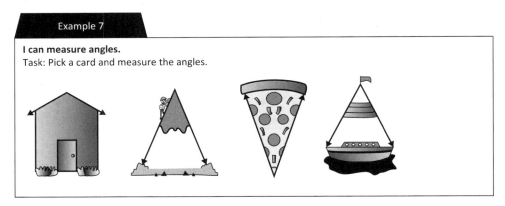

Example 7

I can measure angles.
Task: Pick a card and measure the angles.

Triangles Workstations

Students should have experience with a variety of triangles. Too often, upper elementary students do not get to work with these ideas in more than one way. They should be making different types of triangles, going on triangle hunts, and discussing them in complex ways through scaffolded organizers (see Figures 11.19, 11.20, and 11.21).

Concept: There are a variety of triangles with different attributes and properties.
Workstation: Recognize, draw, and build different triangles.

Figure 11.19

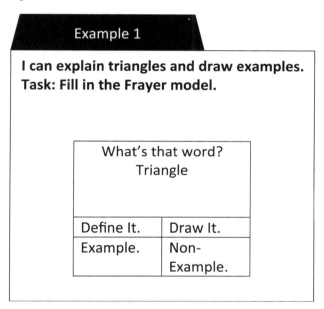

Figure 11.20

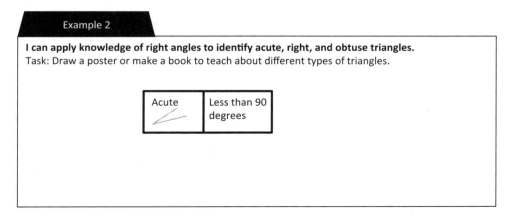

Figure 11.21

Example 3

I can apply knowledge of right angles to identify acute, right, and obtuse triangles.

Task: Make a poster about different types of triangles.

Symmetry Workstations

Symmetry is something that provides many opportunities to have different experiences with. Students can paint pictures, work with pattern blocks, build geometric figures with Play-Doh, and other things.

Concept: Reflection symmetry means that one half is the exact reflection of the other half.
Workstation: Recognize, draw, and build 2D symmetrical shapes (see Figure 11.22).

Figure 11.22

Example 1	
I can build symmetrical pictures. **Task:** Use the pattern blocks and sticks to build symmetrical pictures.	*I can recognize lines of symmetry for a 2D figures.* **Task:** Cut symmetrical shapes out of paper and use them to make an illustrated book about the symmetry of polygons.
I can draw lines of symmetry. **Task:** Draw several shapes with your geometry template and draw different lines of symmetry on those shapes.	*I can recognize lines of symmetry for a 2D figure.* **Task:** Make shapes out of Play-Doh and cut lines of symmetry onto those shapes.

Congruency and Similarity Workstations

These are topics that students can also explore in a variety of ways. They should have to build and make different objects that are either similar or congruent because then it is a concrete way of knowing rather than just pictorial (see Figures 11.23, 11.24, and 11.25).

Figure 11.23

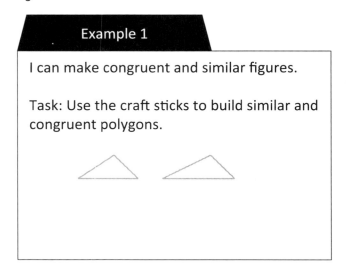

Example 1

I can make congruent and similar figures.

Task: Use the craft sticks to build similar and congruent polygons.

Figure 11.24

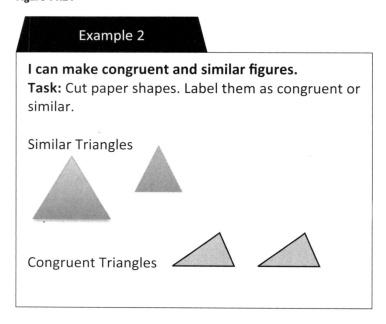

Example 2

I can make congruent and similar figures.
Task: Cut paper shapes. Label them as congruent or similar.

Similar Triangles

Congruent Triangles

Figure 11.25

Example 3

I can make congruent and similar figures.
Task: Build congruent and similar polygons on the
geoboard. Copy your figures onto the geoboard paper.

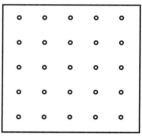

Coordinate Plane Activities Workstations

Concept: Coordinate grids are grids which have points that can be found using their coordinates on the x and y axis.
Workstation: Students can plot points on a coordinate grid.

There are plenty of games to teach students how to start plotting points on the coordinate grid. I usually read the story *A Fly on the Ceiling* by Julie Glass and Richard Walz, which is a math myth about how Descartes came up with the idea of a coordinate grid. I have the students put money at different points on the grid. Then they have to roll the dice and find the coordinate pair. If there is money on the pair, they get to keep it. Whoever gets the most money after ten rolls wins the game.

Culminating Activities

At the end of the unit, it is important to do a lot of activities. It is important to have activities to prepare them for the chapter and state tests and then other ways for students to show their understanding. Many of these activities can be done with partners and in groups (see Figures 11.26, 11.27, 11.28, and 11.29).

Figure 11.26

Choice Board		
You must choose two things from the board to do by the end of the unit. You can work on these projects in your workstations and at home. Please submit your plan to Ms. Thomas by next Wednesday, February 18th. Be sure to look at the specific rubric for your projects.		
Make a poster about triangles.	Make a Glog about geometry.	Design your own project about lines.
Make a board game to practice 2D and 3D shapes.	Write an essay about shapes in real life. Use numbers, words, and pictures.	Make a PowerPoint about 2D figures.
Do the *Find Someone Who Can* board about lines.	Make a board game to practice geometry.	Make a podcast about geometry.

Figure 11.27

My Plan for Geometry Projects

Week 1:
First, I will work on the poster project. I am going to do this by myself. I will do this in the Vocabulary/Writing workstation.

Week 2:
Then I will work on the board game about lines and angles. I will also do this in the Geometry workstation. I am going to design the game in a group.

Figure 11.28

Geometry: Find Someone Who...		
I understand geometry. I can discuss different geometry topics. Task: During project choice time, take the board and find different people to fill in your board. Each person must sign their name and prove that they can do the task. They can either write it on the board or on another piece of paper. Each person can only answer one time.		
Write down four quadrilaterals. Signature:	Draw a Venn diagram to show and discuss quadrilaterals. Signature:	Make and discuss three different types of angles with your arms. Signature:
Explain parallelograms. Signature:	Make two different 3D shapes out of Play-Doh. Signature:	Name and sketch two quadrilaterals that are not parallelograms. Signature:
Draw three different types of triangles and discuss them. Signature:	Talk about shapes in real life. Signature:	Find different types of lines in the classroom and discuss them. Signature:

Figure 11.29

True or False Sort
I can sort statements about geometry. Task: Pick a card. Decide whether or not it is true or false. Sort them. Turn them over and verify if you are correct or not.

All triangles measure 180 degrees.	All quadrilaterals are parallelograms.	All rectangles are squares.

True	False

Teaching in the 21st Century

There is a plethora of tools that students can use to understand geometry (see Figure 11.30). Be sure to read the books about geometry and do some of the activities in the books. Teach some of the songs. Be sure to download the pattern blocks and tangrams and the pattern block paper so they can represent shapes with these tools. Have the students play some of the internet games as well.

Figure 11.30

Resources for Teaching Geometry			
Picture Books	**Videos**	**Virtual Tools**	**Internet Games**
Shapes	**Shapes**		**Shapes**
Grandfather Tang's Story by Ann Tompert	The Greedy Triangle https://www.youtube.com/watch?v=dnZHVFMESJA	https://illuminations.nctm.org/Activity.aspx?id=3521	http://www.mathplayground.com/matching_shapes.html
The Greedy Triangle by Marilyn Burns			**Angles**
If You Were a Polygon by Marcie Aboff	Spaghetti and Meatballs for all https://www.youtube.com/watch?v=jN_GmgeU5cw	http://illuminations.nctm.org/activity.aspx?id=3577	http://www.mathplayground.com/alienangles.html
Angles			**Area and Perimeter**
Sir Cumference and the Great Knight of Angleland: A Math Adventure by Cindy Neuschwander			http://www.mathplayground.com/area_perimeter.html
Area and Perimeter	**Angles**		http://www.mathplayground.com/PartyDesigner/PartyDesigner.html
Spaghetti and Meatballs for all by Marilyn Burns	https://www.brainpop.com/math/geometryandmeasurement/angles/		
Chickens on the Move by Pam Belviso Pollack	https://www.youtube.com/watch?v=vB9Fax-9nAs		**Coordinate Grids** A fly on the ceiling https://www.youtube.com/watch?v=HfecU1nqKFc
*Article about teaching geometry http://gse.buffalo.edu/org/buildingblocks/writings/yc_ideas_shapes.pdf	**Area and Perimeter** https://www.youtube.com/watch?v=qU8aWpRd6Qw		

Key Points

- Classify shapes
- Compose and decompose shapes
- Lines
- Triangles
- Coordinate grids

Summary

Geometry is an important subject that requires many different hands-on experiences. Students need to be able to recognize, identify, draw, analyze, compare, and classify lines, angles, and figures. They should have many opportunities to build, sketch, draw, and paint different shapes. They need ample opportunities to discuss and justify their thinking using numbers, words, and models.

Reflection Questions

1. What are three different tools that you use to teach geometry?
2. Do you use Play-Doh, craft sticks, toothpicks, and other materials?
3. How often do you have students identify geometric ideas in real life?

References

Charles, R. (2005). Big ideas and understandings as the foundation for elementary and middle school mathematics. *NCSM Journal of Mathematics Education Leadership*, 7(3).

Clements, D. and Sarama, J. (2000). Young children's ideas about geometric shapes. *Teaching Children Mathematics* (April). Retrieved from http://gse.buffalo.edu/org/buildingblocks/writings/YC_Ideas_Shapes.pdf on March 26, 2016.

Part IV

Assessment

12

Math Workstation Assessment

> In an effective classroom, students should not only know what they are doing, they should know why and how.
>
> —Wong and Wong (1991)

Balanced assessment is an integral part of successful math workstations. Pre-assessments help to guide where students will go and what they will work on. The ongoing assessments help to guide the instruction throughout the unit of study. Anecdotals and checklists are important guideposts for where students are as well. The final assessments give information about what should be done next. This chapter will discuss balanced assessment as it relates to math workstations.

Pre-Assessment for Math Workstations

Pre-assessments tell you who goes where and what they should be doing when they get there. There are many different kinds of ways to pre-assess. Three of the top ways are a pre-assessment quiz, questionnaire, and interview (see Figures 12.1, 12.2, 12.3, and 12.4).

Pre-assessment Quizzes

A pre-assessment quiz should test the prerequisite skills for the chapter because it allows the teacher to know if there are any gaps to fill. Many times, there are gaps between the current grade level standards and the prior skills. It is important to know what the gaps are so that they can be addressed and the teaching of the new skills goes smoothly. Many times, pre-assessments are made that only test the current grade level standards. These are great for growth measures but tell you nothing of the gaps. Make gap tests so you can make sure that students are ready to grow to the next step.

Figure 12.1

Example 1

Multiplication Pre-Assessment

1a. What is the total number of hamburgers?

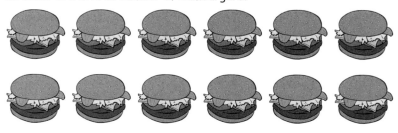

—— Hamburgers

1b. Which equation matches the picture above?
a. 3 + 3 + 3 + 3
b. 4 + 4 + 4
c. 3 + 4
d. None of the above

2. Draw an array that matches this expression.
       2 + 2 + 2 + 2
3. Draw an array that shows 8 marbles.
4. Write a repeated addition equation that shows the total number of ice cream scoops.

5. What is 1 × 0? _____

6. What is 2 × 5? _____

7. Write something that you know about multiplication. Use numbers, words, and pictures.

Figure 12.2

Example 2

1. Write everything you know about fractions.

2. What is easy?

3. What is tricky?

Figure 12.3

Example 3

1. What is division? Explain what you know using numbers, words, and pictures.

2. What is easy about division?

3. What is tricky about division?

4. What do you need to study more to get better with division?

5. What do you want to learn about division?

Figure 12.4

```
Example 4

1.  Tell me three things you know about division.

2.  Write and solve a division word problem.

3.  Do you find division easy, hard, or in-between?
```

Ongoing Assessment of Math Workstations

Throughout the workstation activity, students will be doing work that they should keep track of. They should have a workstation folder that holds all of their activity sheets. Remember that worksheets are often not as academically rigorous as activity sheets (see Figure 12.5). The activity sheet is where they are recording their work, their thinking, the activities they are doing. A worksheet is where students are all doing the same thing at the same time. Even if different students get different worksheets, this doesn't really give the same impact as an activity sheet.

Activity Sheets versus Worksheets

Figure 12.5

```
Example 1

Activity Sheet                         Worksheet

I can compare fractions.        Compare the fractions with
Partners pull fractions and     a symbol.
compare them with
symbols. Record your work.      1/2          1/4

_____    _____             _____      _____

_____    _____             1/4          3/4

_____    _____             _____      _____

                                7/8          6/9

                                _____      _____
```

Anecdotals

Teachers should also spend time watching students work in workstations and taking anecdotal notes of what they are doing. These can be done on Post-its, index cards, or some sort of paper filing system (see Figures 12.6 and 12.7).

Figures 12.6 and 12.7

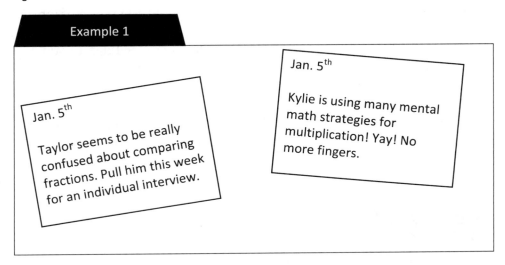

Checklists

Checklists are an efficient way of recording what is happening in the workstations. There are teacher checklists and then student checklists (see Figures 12.8 and 12.9). There are checklists for different things. Two important categories are fluency and word problems.

Portfolio Pieces from Math Workstation

A portfolio is an intentional, thoughtful, representative collection of student work. Students should be encouraged in every unit of study to select a few pieces of work that demonstrate understanding and include it in a portfolio of that unit. For example, there might by two to four items in the portfolio, two teacher selected and two student selected. These items can come from different activities and projects done at the workstation. The teacher and the student are each required to pick two items; however, there can be some overlap in the choices. For example:

- Teacher selected (should be the item and an explanation of why it was chosen)

- **Fractions Vocabulary Poster**—I chose this item because Carol really demonstrated an understanding of fraction vocabulary. The explanations and the examples were thorough, clear, and well done.
- **Quick Essay**—I chose this item because Carol demonstrated with numbers, words, and pictures that she thoroughly understood fractions.
- Student Selected (should be the item and an explanation of why it was chosen)
  - **Crossword Puzzle**—I chose this item because I did a good job. It was really hard to make the definitions, and Jose and I worked really hard to do it well. I am proud of our crossword puzzle and our classmates liked it too.
  - **Podcast**—I think we did a good job of explaining how we use fractions in real life. We gave three examples that made sense.

Figure 12.8

Example 1

Division Strategy Checklist

Name _____

Date _____

☐ I can divide 0 by any number.

☐ I can divide any number by 1.

☐ I can divide by 10.

☐ I can divide by 5.

☐ I can divide by 2.

Name _____

Date _____

☐ I can use the "think multiplication" strategy when I am dividing.

☐ I use other strategies when dividing.

☐ I just know it!

Figure 12.9

Example 2

3rd Grade Word Problem Checklist

Name _____

Date _____

☐ Can solve all addition types.

☐ Can solve all subtraction types.

☐ Can solve all multiplication types.

☐ Can solve all division types.

☐ Can solve all types of one-step problems.

☐ Can solve all two-step problems.

☐ Can solve elapsed time problems.

☐ Can solve mass problems.

☐ Can solve volume problems.

☐ Can solve one- and two-step bar graph problems.

☐ Can solve real word problems about perimeter and area.

Evaluating Assessment of Math Workstations

It is important that teachers take the time to evaluate their workstations at the end of every unit. This should be done by reflecting on a series of questions:

- What is working well?
- What might be changed?
- What should I do differently next time and why?

Reflection on workstations should also be done by having the students talk about how the workstations are helping them to learn. Think about these ideas and ask the students either verbally, in written form, as a small group or classroom discussion, or a mix of these.

- What do the students think about the workstations?
- Do they feel they are learning anything in the stations?
- ·Would they like to change anything?

Key Ideas

- Pre-assessment
- Ongoing assessment
- Anecdotals
- Checklists
- Evaluating workstations

Chapter Summary

There should be many ways to provide evidence that students are actually building conceptual understanding, practicing procedural fluency, reasoning, and building strategic competence. Students need an opportunity to reflect on the work they are doing as well. Pre-assessments, anecdotals, checklists, and self-reflections all help teachers and students know where they are so they can better plan where they are going.

Reflection Questions

1. Do you have a variety of ways to assess what is happening in the workstations?
2. Do you ever ask your students how they are feeling about their learning in the workstations?
3. What do you do really well in terms of assessment and what could you work on?

Reference

Wong, H. K. and Wong, R. T. (1991). *The first days of school: How to be an effective teacher*. Mountain View, CA: Harry K. Wong Publications, Inc.

Appendix A

An Action Plan for Making It Happen

A plan without a date is a dream. . . . Set some dates . . . now!

Introduction to Action Planning for Math Workstations

The point of this chapter is to think about where you are and where you want to be in what specific time frame. It is also to begin to plot out how you are going to get there. Action planning means that you are going to make a step-by-step plan that you will follow and do. It's different than a list. A list can sit there for years. A plan has dates to make the dream come true.

Identify and Prioritize Your Math Goals

The way to identify and prioritize your math goals is to look at the data. Where is your data? How current is it? What part of it are you going to start with (of course, it is all important, but you must start somewhere). I highly recommend that you start with your fluency data and then proceed to the word problem data. These are the areas of highest need on all standardized tests across the country.

Steps:

Use this template or make one. Have some sort of organizer that is written.

  a. Look at data.
  b. Pick a focus area.
  c. Pick a time frame (timelines matter—they are the difference between *woulda, coulda, and **did***).
  d. Make a plan (step by step).
  e. Start small (little steps help you to move great distances).

Figure A.1

Action Plan							
Specific Goal? What do you want to achieve? Why? How is it relevant to improving student achievement?	What data are you going to start with to inform that goal?	Timeframe (specific dates)	Tasks (step by step)	Milestones (define milestones and schedule for each action step)	Challenges (define all potential challenges and describe how to tackle them)	Effect/ Results (What outcome is expected of each action step?)	Success Criteria (What does it look like? How will you know?)

Figure A.2

A Questionnaire to Get You Started:

1. Where will you begin?

2. When you visualize workstations in your classroom, what do you see?

3. What's the first step to making that happen?

4. What data will you use to group your students?

5. Will you have workstations that rotate or are stationary? Why?

6. What management system (schedule board) do you think will work best for you?

7. What are you going to use to store the workstations?

8. How are you going to debrief the workstations with the students daily/weekly?

9. What are you most excited about?

10. What do you still have questions about? (email drnicki7@gmail.com)

Appendix B
Guidelines and FAQs

Here Are Some General Guidelines for Great Workstations

1. Organization is the key. Everything must be organized and labeled.
2. Focus. It is much better to have a few workstations with powerful activities than a bunch of workstations full of worksheets that demand to be changed all the time.
3. Start with what they know. At the beginning of the year practice the focus standards from last year. Teach social skills and routines and then add new grade-level appropriate content. Always review the priority areas and gaps from the prior year.
4. Take the first 20 days to get it going. Invest the time.

FAQs

1. **How do I get started? What do I do first?**
   Start with the students. Where are they? What do they know? Are there any gaps in their knowledge or skill base for the priority standards?

2. **How many workstations should I start with?**
   One. Plain and simple. Don't rush in only then to rush out. One station is sufficient to get started. Do one well. After that, add. Start with either fluency or word problems because both of those are easy to assess, determine levels, and then set up data-driven spaces to work.

3. **What's the best way to organize them?**
   Any way you want. There is no best way. Whichever way preserves your personal sanity. For me, that's portable workstations that

move. I don't like the students having to move around so much. I think there is too much potential to waste precious instructional minutes. Other people disagree with me. They argue that it gives the students a brain break. I agree. So, just choose what works for you. Do that.

4. **How do I know they aren't just faking me out (pretending to work while really doing nothing.)**

   Planning. If you plan for the work, monitor the work through accountability structures like task recording sheets, and then actually use them and discuss them with students, then they will be accountable. But also, engagement is a key factor. If your students *want to play the game*, then they are much more likely *to play the game*. Remember that Mary Poppins said, "A spoonful of sugar helps the medicine go down." Also, and most importantly, what you permit, increases. What you plant, will grow. So, in the beginning of the year, take those first 20 days and plant organization, accountability, and hard work! It will pay off all year long.

5. **Do students really learn this way?**

   Yep, they sure do! Listen to some voices from the field:

Alison:	*"Using Math Workstations has transformed our math classrooms by empowering teachers to truly meet the individual needs of students and creating an atmosphere of independence and enthusiasm. Students love taking control over their learning and are much more in tune to the purpose of the activities and what the math is. It's a brilliant model because students get exactly what they need, enjoy the variety of experiences, and have the opportunity to be challenged at just the right level. Math Workstations are the antithesis of 'one size fits all' instruction and have really shifted how both our teachers and students perceive math class."*
Ann Elise:	*"Implementing workstations as part of my math instruction was simply transformational for my classroom! Student engagement skyrocketed and allowed me to implement unparalleled differentiated instruction. Rather than being someone imparting knowledge, I became a facilitator helping each student find success on their math journey."*
A Chicago student:	*"Workstations are fun. Sometimes hard but fun. You get to play with your friends."*

Resources

Snap cubes and unifix cubes: www.teacherspayteachers.com/Store/Chelsea-Schoeck

Pattern blocks:

Figure B.1

Number lines:

Figure B.2

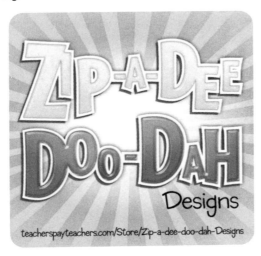

http://www.teacherspayteachers.com/Store/Zip-a-dee-doo-dah-Designs

Jason's Online Classroom: https://www.teacherspayteachers.com/Store/Jasons-Online-Classroom

Dice and clocks: http://www.teacherspayteachers.com/Store/A-Little-Peace-Of-Africa

Figure B.3